SIR JOHN FRANKLIN'S EREBUS AND TERROR EXPEDITION
LOST AND FOUND

GILLIAN HUTCHINSON

ADLARD COLES NAUTICAL

B L O O M S B U R Y

LONDON · OXFORD · NEW YORK · NEW DELHI · SYDNEY

Adlard Coles Nautical
An imprint of Bloomsbury Publishing Plc

50 Bedford Square   1385 Broadway
London   New York
WC1B 3DP   NY 10018
UK   USA

www.bloomsbury.com
www.adlardcoles.com

ADLARD COLES, ADLARD COLES NAUTICAL and the Buoy logo are trademarks
of Bloomsbury Publishing Plc

First published 2017

British Library Cataloguing-in-Publication Data
A catalogue record for this book is available from the British Library.

Library of Congress Cataloguing-in-Publication data has been applied for.

ISBN: PB: 978-1-4729-4869-4
ePDF: 978-1-4729-4870-0
ePub: 978-1-4729-4871-7

2 4 6 8 10 9 7 5 3 1

Typeset in Noto Serif by Lee-May Lim
Printed and bound in China by Toppan Leefung Printing

Bloomsbury Publishing Plc makes every effort to ensure that the papers used in the manufacture
of our books are natural, recyclable products made from wood grown in well-managed forests.
Our manufacturing processes conform to the environmental regulations of the country of origin.

To find out more about our authors and books visit www.bloomsbury.com. Here you will find extracts,
author interviews, details of forthcoming events and the option to sign up for our newsletters.

In association with Royal Museums Greenwich, the group name for the National Maritime Museum,
Royal Observatory Greenwich, Queen's House and *Cutty Sark*.

CONTENTS

PREFACE

Sir John Franklin set out with HMS *Erebus* and HMS *Terror* in 1845 on a voyage to find the North-West Passage. The ships disappeared into the Arctic, never to be seen again until their wrecks were discovered in 2014 and 2016.

This brief guide fills in the background to Franklin's expedition and describes the attempts that have been made to find survivors and discover what happened. Mystery still remains, however. Will examination of the shipwrecks solve it?

FOREWORD

The 1845 expedition to the Arctic, commanded by Sir John Franklin, was the largest, best-equipped expedition that Britain ever sent north, yet it ended in tragedy. Back home, the deaths of its 129 men devastated families. The disaster was writ large upon the Victorian imagination, represented in art, theatre and music. Exactly what happened is still subject to speculation.

The objects that Franklin searchers brought back were displayed in the Painted Hall in Greenwich from the 1850s. They were literally brought over the road when the National Maritime Museum opened in 1937 and have been important to the Museum ever since. We are grateful to Greenwich Hospital, the Gell Muniment Trustees, the descendants of Leopold McClintock and others for the things that they have entrusted to us over time. All these objects remain enigmatic witnesses to the final days of Franklin and his crew.

The finds of HMS *Erebus* and HMS *Terror* are some of the most exciting maritime archaeological discoveries of recent years. Those who cooperated so successfully in locating them are to be congratulated. We are grateful to Parks Canada for lending some of the material recovered from the wrecks, and to the Government of Nunavut for allowing them to travel back to Britain for the first time, for display in the first major exhibition since the ships' discovery, *Death in the Ice: The Shocking Story of Franklin's Expedition*, at the National Maritime Museum from 14 July 2017 to 5 January 2018. Much of the material in this book will also go on display in the National Maritime Museum's new Polar Worlds gallery from 2018 onwards. Now, tantalisingly, the possibility of further explanation for the crews' deaths exists.

It has been an enormous pleasure to work in collaboration with the Canadian Museum of History, sharing mutual expertise and collections to produce the *Death in the Ice exhibition*. The Canadian High Commission in London has also been a stalwart source of help. As Canada celebrates the 150th anniversary of its Confederation, we are delighted, through the exhibition, to be able to demonstrate the strong ties between our two nations, both past and present.

Dr Kevin Fewster AM
Director, Royal Museums Greenwich

CHAPTER 1

THE NORTH-WEST PASSAGE

◄ **1.1 Globe of the world (detail),** Malby & Co, 1845

The aim of Sir John Franklin's *Erebus* and *Terror* expedition was to find a North-West Passage – a sailing route from the Atlantic Ocean to the Pacific across the top of North America. By the early nineteenth century the British Navy had explored nearly all the oceans of the world and the discovery of a North-West Passage was one of the greatest challenges that still remained.

Captain James Cook, during his third voyage, had been attempting to discover a North-West Passage by entering from the Pacific and sailing east. Cook was killed in Hawaii in 1779, three years into the expedition, and before long the Royal Navy was fully occupied with the American and French revolutionary wars. In 1817, less than 40 years after Cook's death, when Greenland whalers reported that the Arctic ice had thawed to an unusual extent, the British Admiralty decided to resume the search for the passage for a number of reasons.

There was some hope that it might be useful for trade or for moving naval vessels around the world during the brief Arctic summers, with the potential to cut months off the time it took ships to sail from Europe to the west coast of America or China by going all the way round Cape Horn or through the straits of Magellan. It was also thought that the North-West Passage might provide quicker access to the coastal regions of the vast territory held by the Hudson's Bay Company (a fur-trading organisation) on behalf of the British government. National prestige was another motive, since at this time the Hudson's Bay Company ran up against the territory of the Russian-American Company (which operated in Alaska before Russia sold it to the United States later in the nineteenth century), and Britain wanted to show Russia that it was the dominant power in the region. Britain was also keen to enhance its reputation as a world leader in scientific and geographical discovery.

Before Sir John Franklin set out with *Erebus* and *Terror* in 1845, the British Admiralty had sent out a series of expeditions to investigate the Arctic coasts and navigable channels over a period of more than 25 years. The explorers' tracks seemed so tantalizingly close to joining up that Franklin's expedition was confidently expected to make the final breakthrough.

John Franklin had taken part in the very first of the new series of Arctic exploration voyages in 1818. He was commander of one of the ships sent to sail past Spitsbergen, an island in northern Norway, towards the North Pole, while another expedition went to Baffin Bay to explore routes leading west. The Spitsbergen voyage was disappointing. Captain David Buchan in HMS *Dorothea*,

1.1 Globe of the world
Malby & Co, 1845
This globe, claiming to show 'all the recent geographical discoveries', was published on 1 June 1845, less than two weeks after Sir John Franklin's *Erebus* and *Terror* voyage began. The unexplored areas appear to be free of obstructions, giving the impression that completing the North-West Passage should be quite straightforward. Comparison with the NASA image opposite reveals what was still unknown at that time.

▲ 1.2 NASA satellite image of summer Arctic ice coverage
The satellite image reveals landmasses at the south-west end of Lancaster Sound (the main channel entering from the east) that had not been discovered by 1845. It also shows that, even after the dramatic shrinkage of the Arctic ice sheet since Victorian times, any attempt to sail north from Lancaster Sound would be blocked by ice.

accompanied by Lieutenant Franklin in HMS *Trent*, encountered an ice sheet not far north of the island. Although they forced their ships into narrow channels in the ice and made painful progress by using their anchors and windlasses to drag their ships along, the mass of ice ultimately made their mission impossible. Both ships narrowly escaped being wrecked when they were driven against pack ice in a gale.

Meanwhile, Commander Ross in HMS *Isabella* and Lieutenant Parry in HMS *Alexander* charted Baffin Bay. Ross then entered Lancaster Sound on its west side, and sailed westwards for part of a day, with Parry's ship following several miles behind. In the afternoon Ross thought he could see mountains blocking the way ahead and, with the weather deteriorating, he decided to turn back without investigating thoroughly. However, others on board the ship were less convinced that it was a dead end and made their views known to the Admiralty when they returned. As a result,

Edward Parry was sent out again the following year to settle the matter. After entering Lancaster Sound, his two ships, HMS *Hecla* and HMS *Griper*, were able to sail right through the charted locations of the mountains that Ross thought he had seen, proving that they did not exist. Parry's expedition continued westwards, passing the meridian of 110 degrees west of Greenwich and claiming the parliamentary reward of £5,000 for having done so. As winter approached, Parry found a natural harbour for his ships so that they could stay in the Arctic rather than returning home – the first time that British naval vessels had done this. The expedition was therefore in a good position to make an early start in the spring, and the ships succeeded in progressing further westwards before being blocked by ice and having to go back the way they came.

While Edward Parry was exploring by sea, the Admiralty sent John Franklin, along with four other members of the Royal Navy, on an immense overland journey to the shore of the Arctic Sea in order to survey the coast. They set out from Hudson Bay in 1819, walking and travelling by canoe along waterways towards the Coppermine River. The distance was so great that the party took two years to reach the river as it was impossible to travel in winter and they had to spend several months of each year under cover, waiting for the snow to thaw. In summer 1821 Franklin's men, assisted by voyageurs (French-Canadian boatmen) and indigenous guides, worked their way downstream and arrived at the mouth of the Coppermine River, where they launched two large canoes onto the sea. They headed east and succeeded in charting about 550 miles of new coastline. Their return journey was disastrous: at least nine of the 20 men died of starvation and two others were shot dead.

Franklin eventually arrived back in England in 1822, the year after Edward Parry returned to the Arctic on a second voyage with HMS *Hecla* and HMS *Fury*. The aim this time was to enter the Arctic Sea further south than through Lancaster Sound, by finding a passage through the north of Hudson Bay that led to the Arctic coast of North America. The ships found the entrance to a channel, which Parry named Hecla and Fury Strait, but although they overwintered twice they found that it was frozen all year round and they were unable to go through.

➤ **1.3 *Captn Franklin RN, FRS Commander of the Land Arctic Expedition with Fort Enterprise in the background***
Frederick Christian (engraver), after George Robert Lewis, 1824
John Franklin took part in his first Arctic voyage in 1818 and then, in 1819–22 and 1825–27, led two immensely long and arduous overland expeditions to chart the north coast of mainland of North America. In this picture Franklin is shown with surveying instruments, with the winter camp he built in 1820 in the background.

Published for G. Lewis, by Hurst & Robinson, Cheapside, Jan.y 1824.

Drawn by G.R. Lewis

Proof by F. C. Lewis, Southampton Row, Paddington.
Eng.d to H.R.H. the Princ.s Augusta & to H.R.H. the Duch.s of Gloucester.

CAPT.ᴺ FRANKLIN, R.N. F.R.S.

Commander of the Land Arctic Expedition

with Fort Enterprise in the back ground.

In 1824 Parry made a third voyage, again with *Hecla* and *Fury*. He aimed to enter Lancaster Sound then turn south down the first navigable channel, named Prince Regent Inlet. Bad ice conditions prevented the ships from entering the inlet in the first season and the crew had to saw them out of the ice the following July. The ships then made some progress south, but gales and drifting ice drove *Fury* aground and the ship was abandoned, damaged beyond repair. With the crews of both ships now on board *Hecla*, Parry sailed further south and saw clear sea ahead, but decided to turn back to be sure of a safe return.

As Parry was returning home in 1825, Franklin was beginning his second overland expedition to chart the north coast of the mainland. This time he reached the sea by following the course of the Mackenzie River, further west than the Coppermine River, which he had travelled down on his first journey. Having reached the sea, the explorers split into two parties. The party led by John Richardson, who was a doctor and Franklin's second-in-command on both overland expeditions, travelled east to connect the survey to the Coppermine River. Franklin's party went west, crossing Russian America as far as almost 150 degrees west before turning back to rejoin Richardson. Meanwhile, Commander Frederick Beechey in HMS *Blossom* sailed from the Pacific through the Bering Strait and surveyed the coast of the Arctic Sea to a position less than 150 miles from Franklin's furthest point west. Beechey had been a lieutenant in Franklin's *Trent* voyage in 1818 and in Parry's 1819–20 expedition.

Parry's reports of clear sea at the southern end of Prince Regent Inlet enticed Captain John Ross to take leave from the Navy and lead a private expedition to investigate. His reputation had been badly damaged by his mistaken report of mountains blocking Lancaster Sound and he wanted to have another attempt at finding the North-West Passage. With sponsorship from Felix Booth, a gin manufacturer, and partly at his own expense, he set off in 1829 in a paddle-steamer, *Victory*, with a smaller supply vessel, *Krusenstern*. He was accompanied by his nephew James Ross, who had served on all of Parry's voyages. Despite engine problems they made good progress, passing the wreck of HMS *Fury* and sailing 150 miles further south than Parry had done, before anchoring for the winter in an inlet, which they named Felix Harbour in honour of the

◄ **1.4 Captain Sir William Edward Parry (1790–1855)**
Charles Skottowe, *c.*1830
William Edward Parry (always known as Edward) made three voyages in search of the North-West Passage, of which the first was the most successful, sailing west beyond 110 degrees of longitude and so winning a parliamentary prize. He was the first to plan for overwintering in the ice so that his ships could take advantage of more than one sailing season.

⌃ 1.5 John Richardson
Edward Finden (engraver), after T Phillips, RA, 1828
Dr John Richardson was a naval surgeon who accompanied
Franklin on both of his overland expeditions and surveyed a
large portion of the North American coast. Years later, when
Erebus and *Terror* went missing, his loyalty to Franklin was so
strong that he set out overland again to search for him, although
by that time he was over 60 years old.

▲ 1.6 Captain Frederick William Beechey (1796–1856)
George Duncan Beechey, *c*.1822
Frederick Beechey served with John Franklin on his 1818
voyage to Spitsbergen and with Edward Parry on his 1819
voyage into Lancaster Sound. In 1826 Beechey, commanding
HMS *Blossom*, sailed through Bering Strait from the Pacific
and explored the western end of the North-West Passage to
within 150 miles of the furthest point that Franklin reached
on his second overland journey.

▲ 1.7 Sir John Ross (1777–1856)
British school, *c*.1833
John Ross undertook a private expedition in 1829 to follow up
the hopeful lead suggested by Edward Parry's third voyage.
His nephew, James Ross, accompanied him. After their ship,
a paddle-steamer named *Victory*, became trapped in ice, they
survived by reaching the supplies and boats that Parry had
left behind. They were rescued by whalers after spending four
winters in the Arctic.

expedition's sponsor. From there James Ross made sledge journeys
to the west, accompanied by Inuit guides, traversing land that
he named Boothia and crossing a channel to more land beyond.
Thinking that it was a peninsula of the mainland, he named it King
William Land, though it was later found to be an island. He gave
the name Victory Point to the furthest place he reached down its
western side. From there he looked ahead and named the next
headland Cape Franklin after his fellow Arctic explorer, never
imagining that Franklin himself would end up spending the final
months of his life only a few miles away from that point.

◀ **1.8 Commander James Clark Ross (1800–1862)**
John Robert Wildman, 1834
James Ross had served on all of Edward Parry's Arctic voyages. During the 1829–33 *Victory* expedition led by his uncle, John Ross, he determined the position of the North Magnetic Pole using a magnetic dip circle, depicted in this painting. In 1839–43 he commanded *Erebus* and *Terror* on a voyage to explore the Antarctic. When the Franklin expedition disappeared, he led an unsuccessful search in 1848–49.

▼ **1.9 Ross's shelter at Fury Beach**
John Ross, 1829–33
The members of John Ross's expedition abandoned their ship, *Victory*, in 1832 and sledged north to Fury Beach, where they built a house from the wreckage of Parry's ship, HMS *Fury*. This watercolour sketch by John Ross shows the bleak conditions in which they spent the next two winters.

In another sledge journey in 1831, while *Victory* was still frozen in, James Ross succeeded in locating the North Magnetic Pole. After three years of making very little progress it became apparent that *Victory* would never escape the ice, so the ship was abandoned and the expedition members travelled north by sledge to Fury Beach, where they built a house from the wreckage of Parry's HMS *Fury*, repaired *Fury*'s boats and attempted to take them north to Lancaster Sound to look for ships. Ice blocked their way, however, and they returned to Fury Beach and stayed for a further winter, eating the stores Parry had left behind. In spring 1833 they succeeded in taking the boats to Lancaster Sound and were rescued by a whale ship – amazingly, the *Isabella* from Hull, the same ship that John Ross had commanded on his 1818 Arctic voyage. Remarkably, during the expedition's four icebound winters, only three of its 23 members had died.

While Ross and the *Victory* were missing, in 1832 George Back volunteered to go to search for them. Back, also a naval officer, had been on both of Franklin's overland expeditions and had heard

◄ **1.10 Captain Ross and the crew of the *Victory* saved by the *Isabella* of Hull**
Edward Francis Finden (engraver),
after James Ross, *c.*1834
In the summer of 1833, John Ross and his expedition members went to Lancaster Sound in small boats to look out for ships to rescue them. They were overjoyed to see a whaler and amazed to find that it was the *Isabella*, the ship that Ross had commanded in 1818.

◄ 1.11 Captain George Back

S. Russell (engraver), 1836

George Back had been with Franklin on both of his overland expeditions. When John and James Ross failed to return from their voyage in 1832, Back volunteered to go to search for them, following an unexplored river. The men were found, though not by Back, who was then told to keep going with his exploratory journey. In 1836–37 he commanded HMS *Terror* on an unsuccessful voyage to find a route from Hudson Bay to the Polar Sea.

▼ 1.12 Tracks of explorers before Sir John Franklin's 1845 *Erebus* and *Terror* expedition

that the Great Fish River – as yet unexplored by Europeans – ran to the sea somewhere south of Prince Regent Inlet. At a Hudson's Bay Company base, a letter reached him informing him that Ross had been rescued but that he should continue exploring anyway. Back discovered that the river was over 440 miles long, but was obstructed in many places by dangerous rapids and extremely difficult to navigate. Along the way his party had some success in hunting hares, duck and deer.

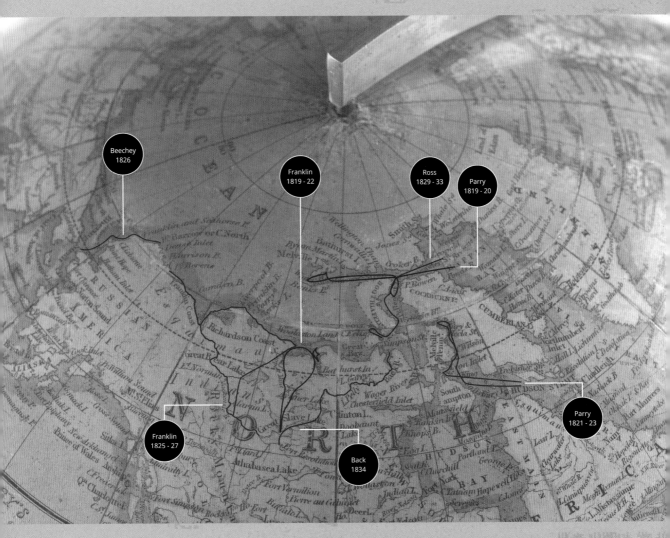

In 1836–39, Hudson's Bay Company explorers Peter Dease and George Simpson led a boat expedition, which charted part of the coast of Russian America west of the Mackenzie River to fill the gap between Franklin's and Beechey's surveys.

The results of all these explorations were used by the Admiralty in planning the orders it issued to Franklin on 5 May 1845 for another expedition to complete the North-West Passage. The orders referred to Parry's success in navigating Lancaster Sound four times and returning 'without experiencing any, or very little difficulty', which gave hope 'that the remaining portion of the passage, about 900 miles, to the Bhering's Strait [*sic*] may also be found equally free from obstruction'. Franklin was therefore to head directly west, without losing time by investigating any openings to the north or south, until he reached Cape Walker, about 98 degrees west. Because Parry's attempt to keep going in that direction had been blocked by a barrier of ice, Franklin was to turn south-west after Cape Walker and try to sail directly towards the Bering Strait.

If progress in that direction was not possible, Franklin was told that he was to consider turning back and attempting to sail north up Wellington Channel if it was clear of ice, as this might give 'ready access to the open sea, where there would be neither islands nor banks to arrest and fix the floating masses of ice'. This apparently bizarre suggestion of heading north if there was too much ice to the south came from a belief in the Open Polar Sea theory. This dated at least as far back as Henry Hudson's Arctic voyage in 1608, when he reported that the further north he went, the warmer the conditions became. The cosmographer Petrus Plancius's explanation for this was that the sun shines on the North Pole for five months of the year, creating a year-round reservoir of heat. He thought that the zone of greatest cold should coincide with the Arctic Circle and that temperatures should rise from there to the pole. Early in the nineteenth century, William Scoresby observed that warm water from the Gulf Stream flows to the west coast of Spitsbergen, and this was taken to support the probability of an ice-free polar sea. The orders went on to say that if neither of the suggested routes allowed the expedition to make the passage during one season, Franklin was to use his judgement either to return home or 'to winter on the coast, with the view of following up next season any hopes or expectations which your observations

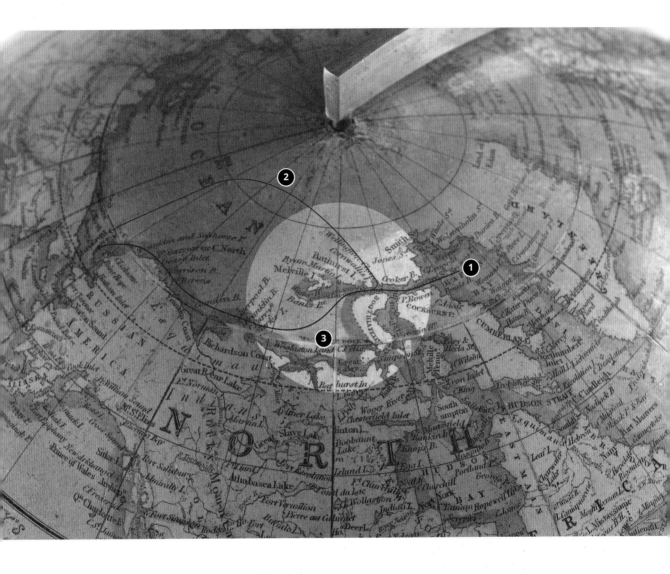

▲ **1.13 The routes recommended in Franklin's orders**

1. Go to Cape Walker then attempt to sail south and west.
2. If that way was blocked, attempt to sail up Wellington Channel to find an open sea route.
3. Failing that, follow up 'any hopes or expectations which your observations … may lead you to entertain'.

this year may lead you to entertain'. His two ships, HMS *Erebus* and HMS *Terror*, should cooperate closely and not separate.

After emerging from the Bering Strait, the expedition was to head south for Cape Horn. On the way, Franklin was to drop off an officer carrying dispatches, who would arrive home first by crossing overland at Panama and taking a passage in a transatlantic ship. The Lords of the Admiralty looked forward to seeing Franklin in the office on his return and learning all about his successful navigation of the North-West Passage.

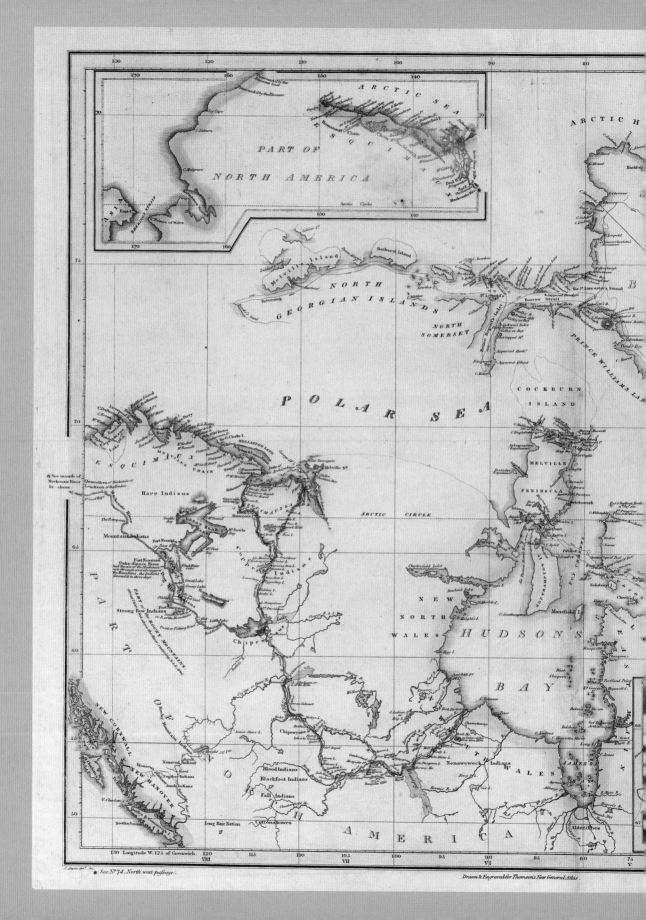

◄ **1.14 Map of the discoveries of Captains Ross, Parry and Franklin in the Arctic regions from the year 1818 to 1827**
Hewitt (engraver), after J Aspin
The public took great interest in the voyages of exploration and publishers had to update their atlases regularly with new maps to show the latest discoveries. This map was created for insertion in Thomson's *New General Atlas*, which had first been published in 1817.

CHAPTER 2

SIR JOHN FRANKLIN

John Franklin was born in Spilsby, Lincolnshire in 1786. Inspired by his first sight of the sea when he was ten, he decided that he wanted a seafaring life and joined the Royal Navy in 1800. Within a few months he was introduced to naval warfare at the Battle of Copenhagen. The following year he sailed as a midshipman on Matthew Flinders' voyage in HMS *Investigator* to chart the coast of Australia. As his cousin, Flinders took a personal interest in John's training in navigation and surveying during the two-year expedition. Afterwards, by which time *Investigator* had become unseaworthy, 60 officers and men sailed for home aboard the *Porpoise*. This ship was wrecked on a sandy reef 200 miles from the Australian coast. Flinders set off with a few men in an open boat to sail the 750 miles to Sydney for help, leaving Franklin and the others camping under sails on the reef, which was just a narrow strip of sand. After six anxious weeks, Flinders returned with rescue vessels.

After Franklin returned from Australia, he became signals officer of HMS *Bellerophon* and was in the thick of the fighting at the Battle of Trafalgar, which he survived without wounds but which left him slightly deaf. He also survived great danger in the War of 1812, between the USA and the United Kingdom, when he led a boat party in an attempt to capture New Orleans. Franklin came through these life-threatening experiences as a devoted Christian with a strong belief that God had protected him.

By the time the wars ended in 1815, Franklin was a lieutenant, but opportunities for employment and promotion were now far fewer. He therefore considered himself very fortunate to have been appointed to the 1818 Arctic expedition, for which he was put in command of a ship for the first time, at the age of 32.

◀ 2.1 *Captain Sir John Franklin, 1786–1847*
William Derby, c.1830
John Franklin's Arctic experience and achievements in 1818, 1819–21 and 1825–27 justified his selection to command the *Erebus* and *Terror* expedition in 1845. This portrait was painted shortly after his second overland expedition.

20

ALEXANDER, 250 Tons, 33 Men.
Lieu.t W.m EDW.d PARRY, Commander.

ISABELLA, 382 Tons, 47 Men.
Captain JOHN ROSS.

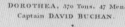

DOROTHEA, 370 Tons, 47 Men.
Captain DAVID BUCHAN.

TRENT, 250 Tons, 33 Men.
Lieu.t JN.o FRANKLIN, Commander.

PORTRAITS OF THE VESSELS ON THE POLAR EXPEDITION OF 1818.

The projecting timbers are for hoisting up the Boats to: but in bad weather they are got on board and laid upon the cross pieces, bottom upward, from bow to stern. The projections are placed two between the fore and main masts, one between the main and mizen, and one at the stern.

Published April 21.st 1818, by J.n Whittle and R.d H. Laurie N.o 53 Fleet Street London.

Captain Buchan on board the *Dorothea* and Lieutenant Franklin on board the *Trent* were ordered to sail to Spitsbergen and then, heading due north, to attempt to reach the North Pole. They were then to sail in a direct line to the Bering Strait to attempt to achieve a North-West Passage. The planning for this expedition was heavily influenced by the Open Polar Sea theory, which postulated that sea temperature increased between the Arctic Circle and the Pole, so that once the ships had broken through the ice sheet north of Spitsbergen they would be in the clear. The orders did say, however, that if the ships were unable to reach the Pole they should attempt to find another way to the Bering Strait.

The expedition was tasked with making observations of magnetic force and seeing how it was affected by 'atmospherical electricity'. John Franklin was excited to be involved in meetings before the expedition departed at which experts discussed the proposed scientific research, and throughout the voyage he made great efforts to observe terrestrial magnetism, atmospheric phenomena, tides and currents, and the depth of the sea.

In the *Trent* Franklin behaved in ways which would cause trouble on his later expeditions. He was happy to take risks by pushing on into dangerous situations without knowing what the outcome would be. He was also so determined not to fail that he pressed ahead despite being aware of serious defects in the expedition's equipment. Before leaving Shetland, the *Trent* was letting in water so badly from an unlocated leak that the seamen had to spend nearly half their watch at the pump. To make matters worse, men from Shetland were unwilling to join the crew and sail in a leaking ship, so Franklin had to set off short-handed. The result was that many of the crew became sick through exhaustion from having to work the windlass so much to haul the ship through the ice, as well as from operating the pumps. The source of the leak was only discovered and repaired several weeks after the ship left Shetland.

After the voyage Captain Buchan commended Franklin for his 'zeal and alacrity', qualities that the Royal Navy held in high regard and which signified an enthusiastic determination to achieve objectives no matter what obstacles and dangers lay in the way. Franklin also won the respect of the men he commanded: the following year, one of the mates, George Back, and a seaman, John Hepburn, went with

◄ **2.2 Portraits of the vessels on the Polar Expedition of 1818:** *Alexander, Isabella, Dorothea, Trent*
James Whittle & Richard Holmes Laurie, 1818
The 1818 polar expedition was a double first for Franklin: it was the first time he had been in command of a ship and the first time he had visited the Arctic. His ship, the *Trent*, is shown at bottom right. Rather than naval ships, the vessels sent to the Arctic in 1818 were whaling vessels that had been bought and strengthened by the Admiralty.

Franklin on his first overland expedition. The other British members of the expedition were naval surgeon John Richardson and midshipman Robert Hood, a talented artist.

In winter 1819 the overland expedition stopped at Cumberland House, a small fur-trading depot on the Saskatchewan River. The supplies, guides and interpreters that Franklin had been expecting for the next stage of the journey were not there, apparently owing to rivalry between the Hudson's Bay Company and the North-Western Company, which disrupted the arrangements. The supply situation was no better a thousand miles further on at Fort Chipewyan, though Franklin did succeed in recruiting some voyageurs as porters. He did not consider turning back an option, so in spring 1820 the expedition pressed on with only a day's worth of provisions. The men would have to rely on fishing and shooting to feed themselves, though they were also short of powder for their guns. At Great Slave Lake they met up as planned with a group of indigenous people with canoes who took them northward to a site on the Coppermine River where they could camp for the winter. Franklin named this place Fort Enterprise, and the expedition built log huts there. The plan was to return to it after surveying the sea coast, and Franklin arranged for their guides to lay in supplies for the following winter.

In June 1821 Franklin's party – consisting of 20 men – reached the sea and, despite rough conditions, sailed westwards along about 550 miles of the rock-bound coast. Wanting to go as far as he possibly could, Franklin pushed on late into the season, although provisions were running low. On 18 August they turned back and Franklin decided they would make their way to Fort Enterprise by a different route, following an unexplored river, where he thought there might

be more animals. However, the river turned the wrong way and the men had to cut across country, carrying their canoes, which would be needed when they reached the Coppermine River. The going – across snow lying on top of marshland – was extremely tough. Occasionally the hunters succeeded in killing animals, but for the rest of the time they had to eat rock lichen, which made some of the men vomit. Robert Hood was unable to eat it at all as it made him too ill. Weakened by hunger, the voyageurs had refused to carry the last remaining canoe, so finding another way to cross the Coppermine caused a long delay. The men fought off starvation by eating scraps of leather and rawhide from their clothing and equipment.

▲ **2.3 Gold ring inlaid with wood from Franklin's land Arctic expedition, 1819–22 *c*.1823**
The small piece of wood set into the bezel of this ring is inscribed on the inside: 'part of ye canoe used by Captn Franklin RN in his land Arctic Expedition 1819–22'. The canoes were abandoned during the return stage, so it is a puzzle where this fragment came from and who set it into the piece of jewellery.

▲ 2.4 Moose skin boots, probably of Cree manufacture

These boots made of moose skin were brought home as a souvenir by John Franklin. They may be similar to those he was wearing during his first overland expedition when the starving men resorted to eating anything made of animal skin. As a result of that experience, Franklin became famous as 'the man who ate his boots'.

Franklin sent George Back, who was proficient in using snowshoes, ahead to Fort Enterprise to fetch food while most of the others continued walking as a group to help each other. Robert Hood and some of the others were too weak to go on and Dr Richardson and John Hepburn stayed to look after them. When Franklin's group reached Fort Enterprise they found it deserted and empty, with nothing but rotting deer skins and old bones to eat. George Back had been there and had left again to search for local people. More than two weeks later, Richardson and Hepburn dragged themselves into Fort Enterprise. Richardson announced that Hood was dead, shot through the back of the head by one of the voyageurs, Michel Teroahauté. Richardson had suspected Teroahauté of cannibalising the bodies of other members of the expedition and had shot him to prevent him from turning on Hepburn and himself.

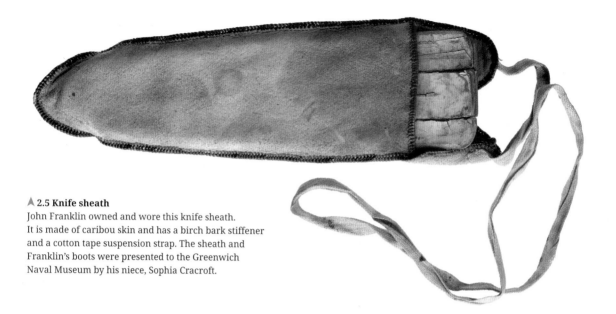

▲ **2.5 Knife sheath**
John Franklin owned and wore this knife sheath.
It is made of caribou skin and has a birch bark stiffener
and a cotton tape suspension strap. The sheath and
Franklin's boots were presented to the Greenwich
Naval Museum by his niece, Sophia Cracroft.

▲ **2.6 Pocket watch**
Griffin & Adams, 1815–16
Robert Hood, the lieutenant on Franklin's first overland
expedition, was too ill to keep up during the return
journey and seaman John Hepburn volunteered to
remain with him. Hood died, murdered by an Iroquois
voyageur, but his father presented Hepburn with this
watch 'As a small token of Gratitude of his great kindness
to his dear Son The late Lieut: Robert Hood. R.N.'

Local people eventually arrived with supplies and
caught fish and game for the expedition members
while they recuperated. Only about half of the party
who explored the coast with Franklin survived.

In July 1822 Franklin, Richardson, Back and Hepburn
sailed for England. Their achievement in travelling
5,500 miles by land and water and their endurance
were celebrated. As he had survived on scraps of
leather, John Franklin became known as 'the man
who ate his boots'. The loss of life added a frisson to
the narrative but did not seem to count against
Franklin, who was now promoted to captain and
elected a Fellow of the Royal Society.

Franklin married the poet Eleanor Porden in the
summer of 1823, by which time he was already
planning another overland journey to follow the course
of the Mackenzie River to the sea and explore the coast
east and west from there. In June 1824 the Franklins'
daughter was born, but Eleanor was by then in the
terminal stages of tuberculosis. She insisted that her
illness should not delay her husband from continuing

△ 2.7 The 'walnut-shell' portable boat carried by Franklin's crew on the 1825–27 overland expedition
British School, 19th century
To solve the problem of crossing rivers, which had caused crucial delays during Franklin's first overland expedition, Colonel Pasley of the Royal Engineers invented the 'walnut-shell boat'. It had a wooden frame and a Mackintosh canvas cover, weighed less than 40 kilograms and could be assembled in less than twenty minutes.

with his exploration work, and he set out in February 1825. Eleanor died a week after he left, but Franklin did not know and continued writing to her until the end of April, when he read of her death in a newspaper.

Franklin was accompanied by his companions from his first journey, John Richardson and George Back, as well as by Lieutenant Edward Kendall. They took three boats, one to carry eight people and two to carry seven, and a party of seamen had been sent on ahead, including one who had been on Franklin's *Trent* voyage, Robert Spinks. The first winter was spent at Great Bear Lake, this time with plenty of supplies, including caribou, moose and trout, and the expedition reached the Mackenzie delta in July 1826. From there, John Richardson led a party travelling east to the Coppermine River and Franklin's party headed west. Franklin had some hopes of meeting up with Captain Frederick Beechey, who had been ordered to sail HMS *Blossom* through the Bering Strait, but that proved impossible.

While exploring the coast, Franklin had an encounter with Inuit that turned hostile. It began with a friendly exchange of items, but a very large group gathered and attempted to take everything from the boats. When Franklin published an account of this incident in his narrative, it helped establish the idea in the minds of the British public that Inuit were a threat to British Arctic expeditions.

Franklin's second overland journey was more successful than the first, in both geographical and organisational terms, and he returned to England in September 1827 with his reputation greatly enhanced. He and Edward Parry were knighted in 1829 in recognition of their Arctic exploration work. The year before, Franklin married Jane Griffin, a friend of his first wife. Perhaps in compensation for years of short rations, his weight increased to 15 stone (95 kg), although he was quite short.

▲ **2.8 Large gold medal of the Société de Géographie, Paris**
Franklin's exploration achievements gained international recognition. The French geographical society struck the first of its large gold medals in 1827 to honour him, and inscribed it: 'To Captain Franklin for his voyages to the polar lands'. The Geographical Society of London was established as a dining club soon after this, in 1830, with John Franklin as one of its founding members.

▶ **2.9 Captn John Franklin RN**
Edward Francis Finden (engraver),
after John Jackson, 1828
Franklin's publisher, John Murray, produced this portrait of him in 1828, showing him as a confident and dashing figure. This was the year in which he married his second wife, Jane, and the year before he received his knighthood.

CAPT.n JOHN FRANKLIN, R.N.

Published by John Murray, London, 1828.

◄ **2.10 The tailcoat of Franklin's civil court dress**
Boggett & Reynolds, 1837
Sir John Franklin wore this on ceremonial occasions when he was lieutenant-governor of Van Diemen's Land (Tasmania), between 1836 and 1844. His difficult experience of colonial administration made him eager to return to sea and polar exploration.

Between 1830 and 1833, during the final years of the Greek War of Independence, Franklin commanded HMS *Rainbow* in the Mediterranean. In 1836 he was appointed lieutenant-governor of Van Diemen's Land (now Tasmania). He worked hard for reform and improvement, but suffered from colonial in-fighting and was undermined by some of his subordinates, especially his colonial secretary, John Montagu. When Franklin sacked him, Montagu complained to Lord Stanley, who agreed that the dismissal had been ill-judged and decided it was time for Franklin to be replaced. The man sent to replace him arrived in Van Diemen's Land four days before Franklin received the notification that he was being recalled. Franklin arrived in London in June 1844, deeply indignant and unemployed, but just as a new Arctic expedition was being contemplated by the Admiralty.

Franklin was immensely keen to lead the *Erebus* and *Terror* expedition. Despite being 58 at the time of applying for the job, he had all the right qualifications in terms of Arctic experience and leadership, and had excellent scientific credentials. Frederick Beechey had also just published a narrative of the 1818 *Dorothea* and *Trent* expedition, which showed him in a good light.

On 7 February 1845 the Admiralty appointed Sir John Franklin to command the *Erebus* and *Terror* expedition.

CHAPTER 3

HMS *EREBUS* AND HMS *TERROR*

The departure of *Erebus* and *Terror* to search for the North-West Passage was a major news story in Britain. Like Sir John Franklin himself, his ships had already been tested by disastrous experiences during polar expeditions, where they and their crews had endured extreme danger, and had shown that they were exceptionally resilient. They were generally thought to be ideal for the expedition. HMS *Terror* was launched in 1813 and HMS *Erebus* in 1826. Both had been strongly built in the first place, as bomb vessels, to take the weight and withstand the recoil of large mortars, used mainly for coastal bombardment. Their formidable names ('Erebus' signifies the darkness at the entrance to Hell) were intended to strike fear into the enemy.

◄ 3.1 *Erebus* and *Terror* setting off to find the North-West Passage
Illustrated London News, May 1845

HMS *Terror* took part in the War of 1812, bombarding American coastal fortifications. After 1815, *Terror* spent the next 20 years idle at Portsmouth and Plymouth except for one brief excursion to the Mediterranean. Then in 1835 there was an exceptionally cold Arctic winter that trapped many British whaling ships in Baffin Bay, and the Admiralty prepared to send HMS *Terror* to the rescue. The comprehensive refit at Chatham dockyard included encasing the ship in an additional layer of planking and strengthening the frames using massive iron and copper fastenings. The hold was divided into watertight compartments so that if the ship did spring a leak, the water would not flood it entirely. To provide buoyancy and stability, the spaces between the compartments and the hull were filled with compacted coal and coal dust so that they could not flood. Storage tanks were fitted into the hold. There was also a pioneering attempt at central heating with the installation of a stove connected to heating pipes.

By the time the work was done, the Baffin Bay whalers no longer needed assistance, but taking advantage of *Terror*'s refit, the Admiralty decided to send an expedition to find out whether there was a sea route from Hudson Bay to the Polar Sea.

▲ **3.2 Model of HMS *Erebus* (1826)**
Admiralty model, *c*.1839
Erebus and *Terror* were bomb vessels, floating platforms for large guns. They were built for strength, not speed, with round, heavy hulls. The two ships were very similar, but *Erebus* was slightly larger than *Terror*. To convert the ships for polar exploration, a massive amount of extra strengthening was built in and projecting parts of the hull were removed. The model shown here has additional planking at the bow and waterline to prevent ice damage.

▲ **3.3 *Perilous position of HMS Terror, Captain Back, in the arctic regions in the summer of 1837***
William Smyth, mid-19th century
HMS *Terror*'s first voyage into the Arctic, in 1836–37, had tested the ship to the utmost. It was trapped in ice floes between August and the following July, and there were several occasions when the crew thought they might have to abandon ship. William Smyth, who painted this picture, was first lieutenant of the *Terror* on this expedition.

Captain George Back's *Terror* expedition set off from Chatham in June 1836 with a crew of 60. They set a straight course through Hudson Strait and past the north-east coast of Southampton Island towards Frozen Strait, but as they approached the Arctic Circle in August, ice closed around the ship, and it was carried along helplessly.

In September it was severely 'nipped' – a gentle-sounding term which actually means being crushed by the immense pressure of the surrounding ice. The thick sheet copper surrounding the galley apparatus began to crumple. Sliding doors refused to shut, and leaks came in through the holes around the hull fastenings so that hourly pumping was necessary. The captain ordered the provisions to be brought up to the deck, ready to be thrown onto the floe in

case the ship began to sink. However, the strength of *Terror*'s hull enabled it to survive, and those seamen who had previous experience of Greenland whaling said that no ship they had ever seen before could have resisted such pressure.

However, this was only a brief respite. *Terror* was completely trapped and was nipped again and again. While the ice creaked and crashed horribly, the ship was squeezed and jerked up by the pressure underneath and violently thrown onto its side. In March the situation reached a crisis. *Terror* was forced up by the ice and thrust backwards with massive shocks. Once again, the crew unloaded the boats and provisions, although if the ship did sink there was no hope of any of them staying alive for long.

By the time the ice melted in July, *Terror* had drifted 200 miles south and east. As the floe broke up, it was discovered that the ship was resting on a deeper iceberg which was pushing the keel up to the surface and tipping the ship, so that its side would soon be submerged. The crew worked frantically to cut through the berg and were rewarded when *Terror* finally righted itself.

The expedition so far had not made any geographical discoveries, and Captain Back did briefly consider pushing on towards Frozen Strait. However, *Terror* was leaking badly, so the men had to work the pumps continuously and they themselves were not in the best condition, perhaps partly due to Back having put them on reduced rations so that they would be able to stay out for a further year if necessary. When the captain told his crew that he had decided that they were now going home, they responded with three hearty cheers.

◄ **3.4** *Situation of HMS* **Terror** *on the 14th July 1837,*
engraving from George Back's *Narrative of an expedition*
in HMS **Terror,** **1838**
L Haghe (engraver), after William Smyth
The ice floe finally broke up in July, but just as everyone was expecting
to be free, it looked as though a submerged iceberg would capsize the
ship. The crew had to cut the ice away before *Terror* could float upright,
'crazy, broken and leaky', as described by Back. Exploration plans were
abandoned and they headed for home.

As *Terror* was passing the coast of Labrador, four Inuit made their way out to the ship through the drift ice and were given some gifts, including a few of the brass medallions, which had been made for that purpose. After the ship cleared Labrador, the return voyage across the Atlantic was very stormy, and although they had been heading for Stromness in Orkney, off the north-east tip of mainland Scotland, Back decided instead to aim for the nearest accessible harbour, which was Lough Swilly in Ireland. The ship was run ashore on a beach to prevent it from sinking at anchor.

When the tide went out at Lough Swilly, it was revealed that a large part of the keel and the sternpost had been wrenched over to one side, leaving gaping holes in the hull. As Back recorded in his narrative of the voyage, 'There was not one on board who did not express astonishment that we had ever floated across the Atlantic.' A team of shipwrights was sent from Chatham dockyard to do enough repairs to get the ship back to England.

▲ **3.5 Medallion commemorating the voyage of HMS *Terror*, 1836–37**
The expedition was supplied with items that could be given as gifts to indigenous people to promote friendly relations with them. Among them were brass medallions like this one, with 'HMS TERROR CAPTN BACK 1836' on one side and an image of Britannia, ruling the waves but holding out an olive branch to show peaceful intentions, on the other.

(PAF 0279)

▲ **3.6 Sketch showing the state of HMS *Terror* on her arrival in Loch Swilly**
Lt Owen Stanley, 1837
HMS *Terror* was leaking so badly on the return voyage across the Atlantic that Captain Back made for the nearest accessible harbour, Lough Swilly in Ireland. This sketch of the extent of the damage was made by Owen Stanley, the second lieutenant on the expedition. Part of the keel and the sternpost had been torn away, but the watertight bulkheads had saved the ship from sinking.

Back's expedition may have been a failure, but the ship was judged to have performed extraordinarily well. So when the Admiralty made plans to send a naval scientific expedition to the Antarctic, HMS *Terror* was chosen along with HMS *Erebus*. *Erebus* was modified in the same way as *Terror* and both ships had their framing and their sterns massively strengthened to withstand the shocks from the ice. Extra pumps were provided and the heating system, which had failed on Back's voyage, was replaced with a better one.

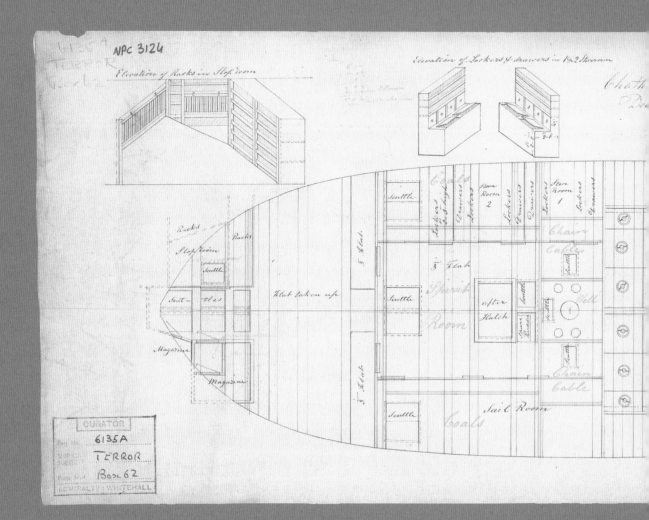

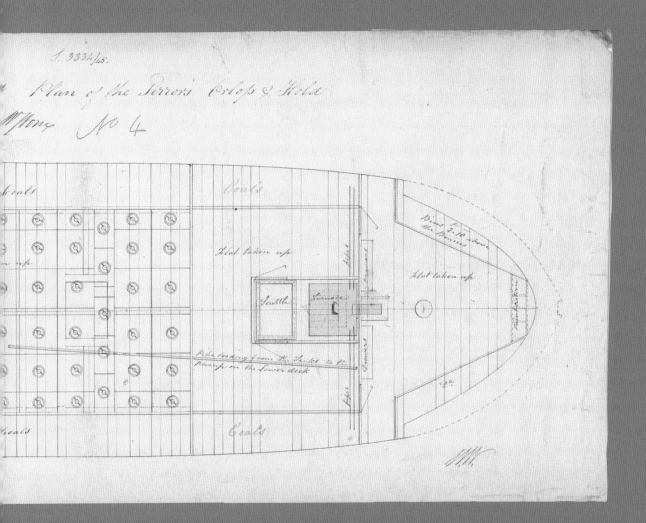

▲ **3.7 Ship plan of *Terror*'s orlop and hold, 1837**
This plan shows the lowest deck (the 'orlop')
and the hold of HMS *Terror*. It is dated
December 1837, when *Terror* was repaired at
Chatham dockyard following Captain Back's
voyage to Hudson Bay. The plan includes
elevations showing new storage furniture.

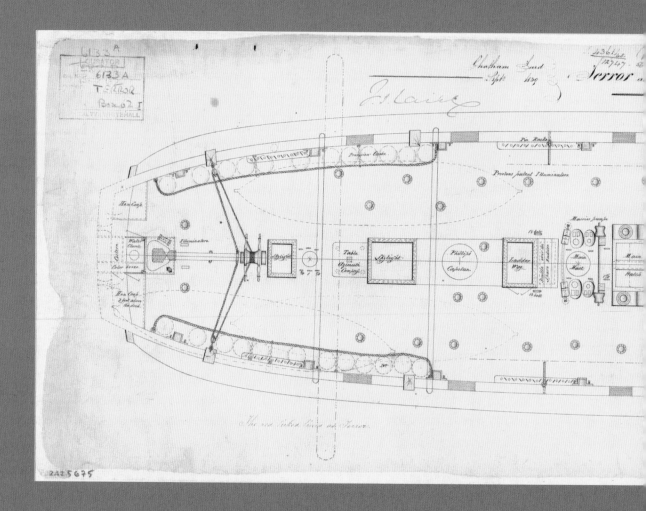

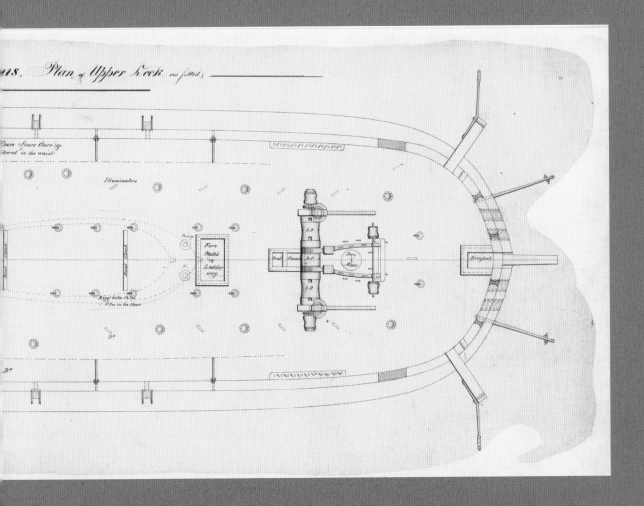

Plan of Upper Deck as fitted,

▲ **3.8 Ship plan showing the upper deck with deck fittings for** *Terror* **and** *Erebus,* **1839**

This plan was drawn in September 1839 when *Erebus* and *Terror* were being strengthened and fitted out in preparation for their voyage to the Antarctic. The two ships were very similar, but *Erebus* was slightly larger, and this drawing shows the position of the bowsprit and hatches as they were on *Erebus* rather than on *Terror*.

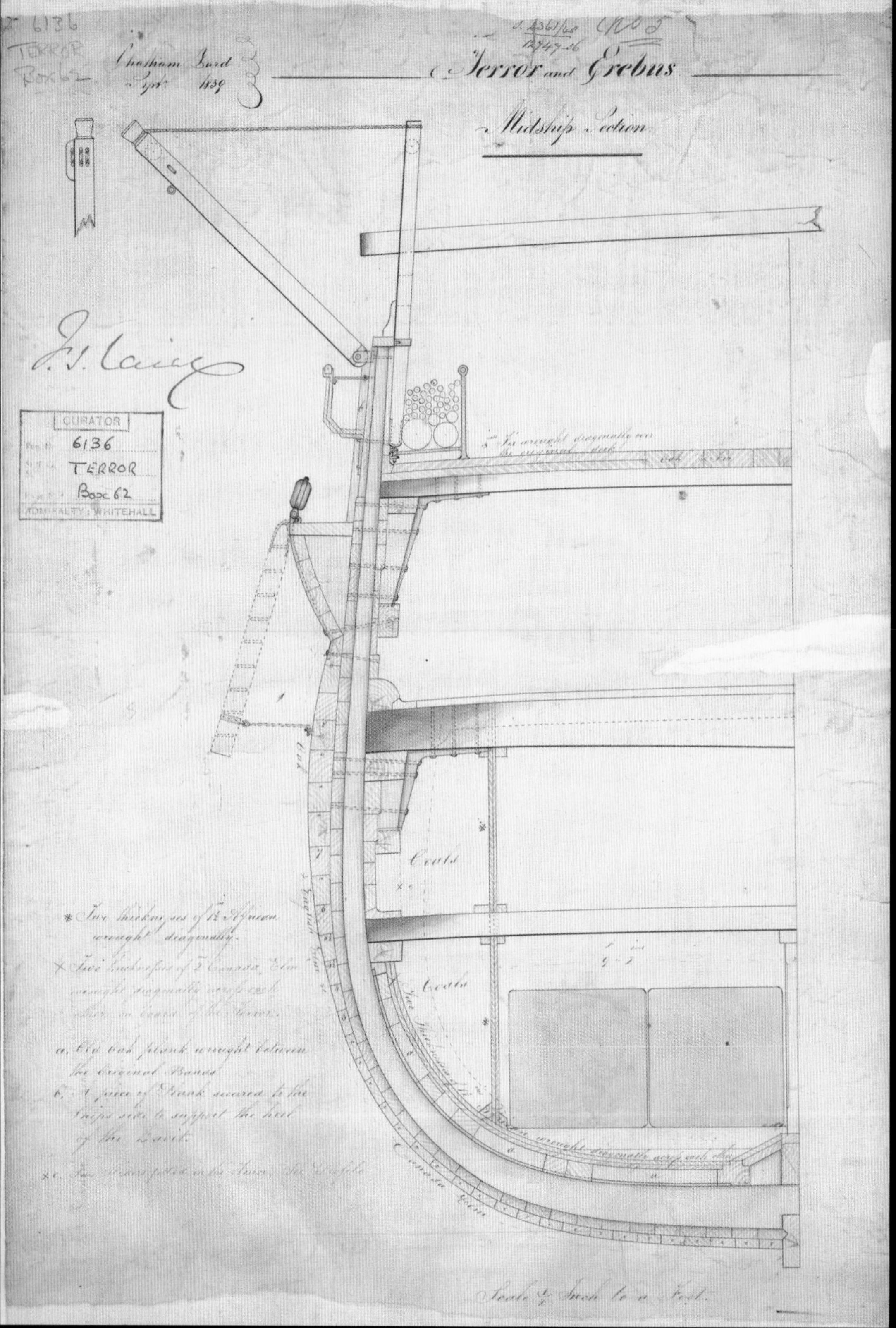

Chatham Yard
Sept. 1839

S. 2361/68
12747.6
No. 5

Terror and Erebus

Midship Section

* Two thickness of R. African
  wrought diagonally.

× Two thicknesses of ⅜ Canada Elm
  wrought diagonally over each
  other, in course of the Terror.

a. Old oak plank wrought between
   the Original Bands

b. A piece of Plank secured to the
   Ships side to support the heel
   of the Davit.

×c. Two Bands fitted in the Store No. Profile

Coals

Coals

Scale ½ Inch to a Foot.

▲ **3.10 *The collision to windward of the chain of bergs,
13 March 1842,* from *A Voyage of discovery and research
in the Southern and Antarctic regions* by Sir James
Clark Ross, 1847**
During Captain Ross's Antarctic voyage, *Erebus* and *Terror*
came close to destroying each other. An iceberg dead ahead
suddenly became visible through heavy snow and *Erebus*
had to turn across *Terror*'s path to avoid it. It was impossible
for *Terror* to clear both the iceberg and *Erebus*, so a collision
was inevitable. The ships crashed violently together and their
rigging became entangled.

◀ **3.9 Plan showing modifications to *Erebus* and *Terror*
before Captain Ross's Antarctic voyage, 1839**
This cross-section diagram specifies the work carried out at
Chatham dockyard to prepare *Erebus* and *Terror* for Captain
James Ross's Antarctic Expedition in 1839. It depicts the
watertight bulkheads, coal-filled compartments and storage
tanks that had proved so effective on Back's voyage and
indicates how the hull was to be fortified with additional layers
of timber.

The Antarctic voyage set out in 1839 with Captain
James Ross commanding in *Erebus* and Captain
Francis Crozier in *Terror,* and returned in 1843.
They sailed into the Antarctic in three successive
years – 1841, 1842 and 1843 – for the purpose of
making discoveries and carrying out observations
of terrestrial magnetism.

Antarctic conditions proved just as challenging as
those in the north, but the ships survived further
perilous incidents. In one of these, they were
caught up in a stormy sea full of rolling fragments
of rock-hard ice, which smashed against them
so violently that their masts shook. Ross thought
that destruction seemed inevitable as the shocks
would have destroyed any ordinary vessel in less
than five minutes. The ordeal lasted 28 hours,
but although the rudders of both ships were
destroyed, their hulls withstood the battering. An
even more dangerous accident occurred in March
1842, when the ships collided with each other
when attempting to avoid crashing into an iceberg.

➤ **3.11 Dockyard plan showing how the propellers of *Erebus* and *Terror* were fitted, 1845**
The sterns of *Erebus* and *Terror* were rebuilt to create a space for attaching the propeller to the engine shaft when power was to be used. The propeller could not be left in place all the time as it would affect sailing performance and might be damaged in the ice. When it was removed, solid chocks filled the space.

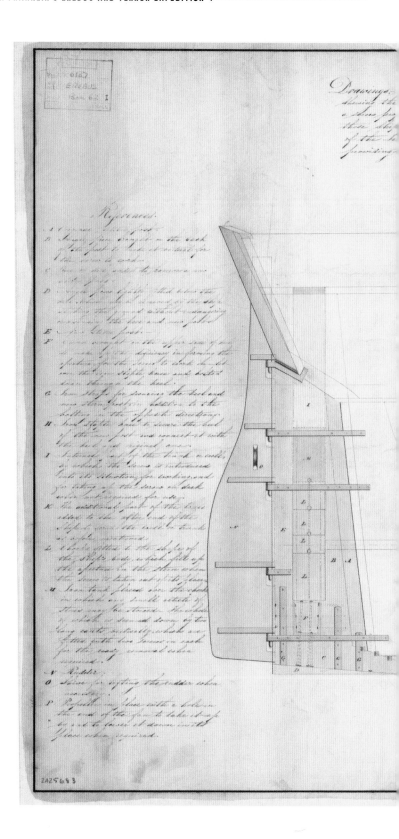

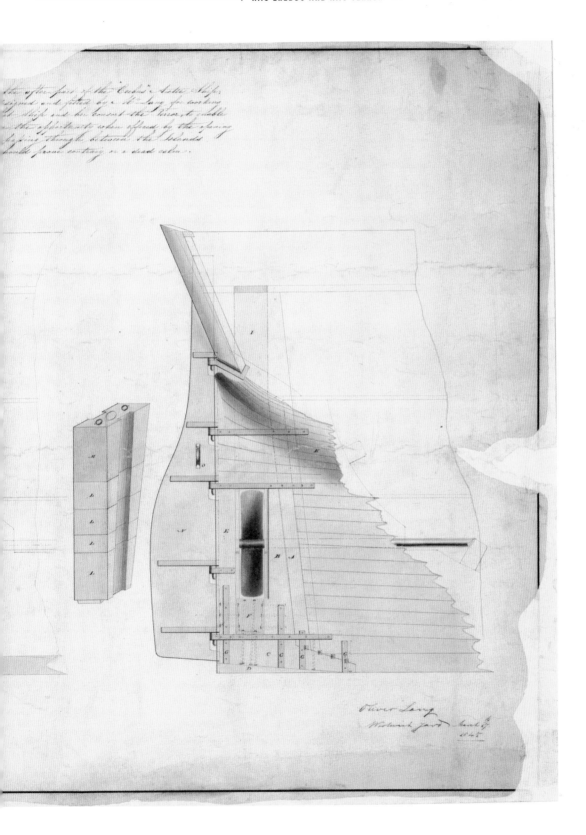

The impact threw the crew members off their feet, while masts and spars snapped and were torn away. The ships were tangled together, rising and falling on the waves at the foot of the iceberg, so that they took it in turns to smash down on each other, splintering the upperworks and the boats. Eventually *Terror* surged past the iceberg and *Erebus* broke free by sailing backwards under mainsail. Thanks to the extra strengthening that had been added to the ships at Chatham, their hulls withstood this extreme test. Both had broken rudders, but they carried spares. *Erebus*'s anchor had been driven deeply into the side of the ship and could not be shifted, until 500 miles later it snapped off in a gale.

A little over a year after their safe return to Britain from the Antarctic, the ships were prepared at Woolwich dockyard for Sir John Franklin's 1845 North-West Passage expedition. They were fitted with new diagonally planked decks and the forward parts of their hulls were cased with iron sheeting. The principal modification was the installation in each ship of a steam engine driving a screw propeller. However, they were both still essentially sailing vessels, and their engines were only intended to be used to make progress through channels between masses of ice, and against the wind where this was necessary. They took enough fuel to power them for only twelve days during an expedition that was expected to last for two or three years, so any decision to fire up the boilers would not have been taken lightly, especially as the funnel and propeller had to be attached on each occasion the engine was used. The propeller had to be let down to its position below the waterline through a well in the stern of the vessel.

The ships' 25-horsepower steam engines had come from railway locomotives. John Irving, the third lieutenant of *Terror*, wrote to his relatives that, in steaming trials on the Thames, the ship had reached a speed of 4 knots (nautical miles per hour) and quipped that 'our engine once ran somewhat faster on the Birmingham line'.

The confidence that the ships inspired is demonstrated by the fact that several men who had already experienced polar voyages in them willingly joined once again for Sir John Franklin's expedition.

➤ **3.12 Captain Sir John Franklin's Cabin Aboard HMS Erebus**
The *Illustrated London News* included this drawing of the captain's cabin in HMS *Erebus* in an account of the departure of Franklin's expedition in May 1845. Two chart lockers can be seen – one containing home and Arctic charts and the other Pacific charts for the voyage from the Bering Strait.

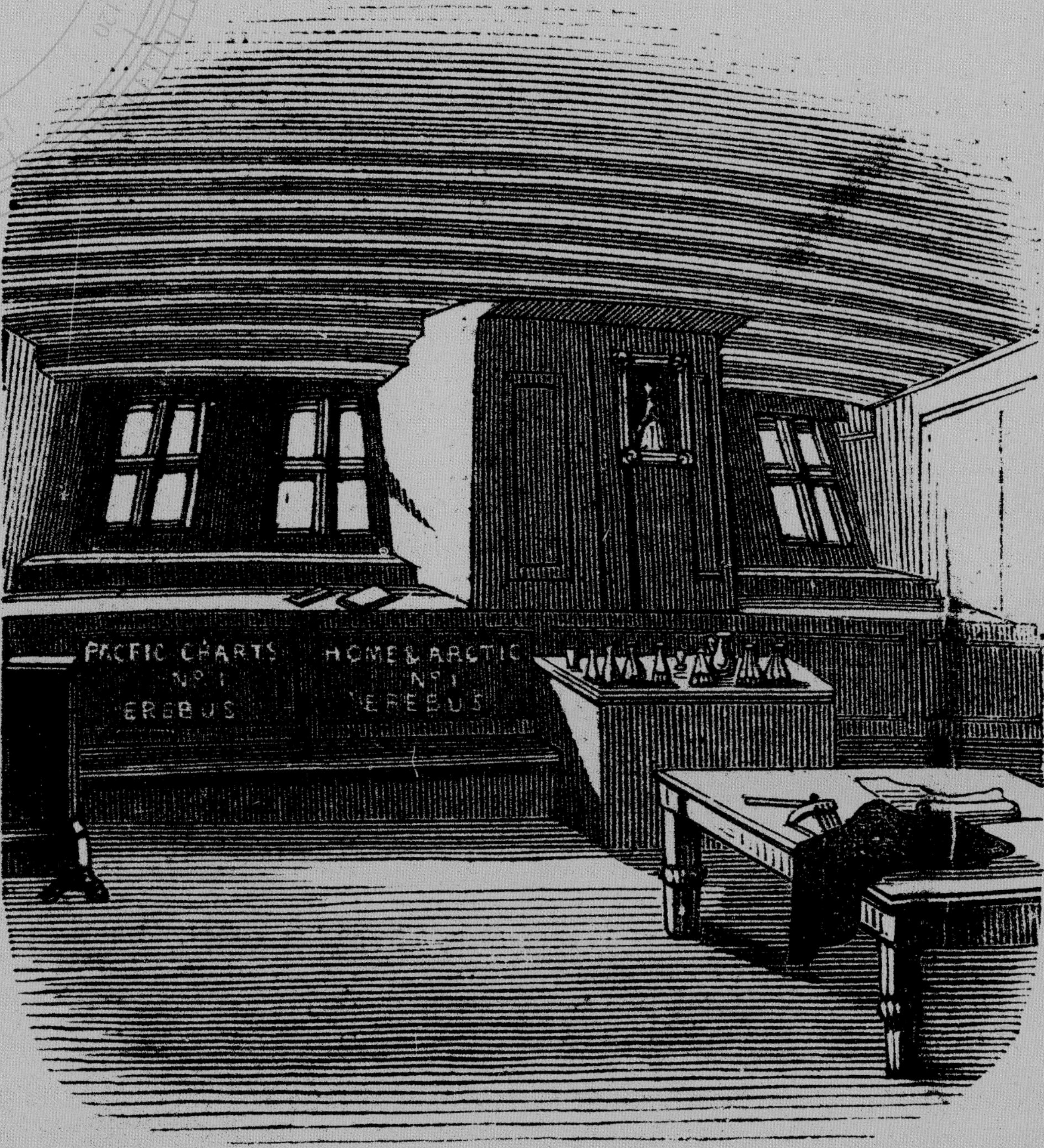
PACIFIC CHARTS
Nº 1
EREBUS
HOME & ARCTIC
Nº 1
EREBUS

Francis Crozier, who had commanded HMS *Terror* in the Antarctic, was its captain again for the Franklin expedition, and six of his former crew accompanied him. Four of *Erebus*'s crew members had also served in that ship in the Antarctic. Graham Gore, first lieutenant in *Erebus*, had also been part of George Back's *Terror* expedition.

With the refit completed, the ships sailed down the River Thames from Woolwich to Greenhithe and departed from there on 19 May 1845. They were accompanied, and often towed, by naval steam ships, while a transport ship, the *Barretto Junior*, carried stores and equipment to be loaded onto the exploration ships in Greenland. They worked their way up the east coast of Britain and

List of Officers, Seamen and Marines of Her Majesty's Discovery Ships "Erebus" and "Terror" who sailed from England May 1845 in the Expedition under the command of Captain Sir John Franklin Kᵗ. KCH

"EREBUS"

Name	Rank			Age
Sir John Franklin KCH	Captain			
James Fitzjames	Commander			
Graham Gore	Lieutenant			
Henry T D Le Vesconte	Lieutenant			
James W Fairholme	Lieutenant			
James Reid	Ice Master			
Stephen S Stanley	Surgeon			
Charles H Osmer	Paymaster & Purser			
Robert O Sargent	Mate			
Charles F Des Voeux	Mate			
Edward Couch	Mate			
Harry D S Goodsir	Assistant Surgeon			
Henry F Collins	Second Master			
Thomas Terry	Boatswain			
John Weeks	Carpenter			
John Gregory	Engineer			
Samuel Brown alas Wm Lately	Boatswains Mate	Hull Yorkshire		
Thomas Watson	Carpenters Mate	Neva Yarmouth Norfolk		40
Philip Reddington	Captain Fore Castle	Brompton Kent		28
Daniel Arthur	Quarter Master	Aberdeen		35
William Bell	Quarter Master	Dundee Forfar		
John Downing	Quarter Master	Plymouth Devon		34
John Murray	Sailmaker	Cadsoe Lancashire		43
James W Brown	Caulker	Deptford Kent		28
William Smith	Blacksmith	Thornton Norfolk		28
James Hart	Leading Stoker	Hampstead Middlesex		33
Richard Wall	Ships Cook	Hull Yorkshire		45
James Rigden	Captain Coxswain	Upper Deal Kent		32
John Sullivan	Captain Main Top	Cottingham Kent		28
Robert Sinclair	Captain Fore Top	Kirkwall Orkney		25
Joseph Andrews	Captain Hold	Edmonton Middlesex		35
Thomas Burt	Armourer	Wrexham Hants		22
Francis Dunn	Caulkers Mate	Llanelly South Wales		25
Edmund Hoar	Captains Steward	Portsmouth Hants		26
Richard Aylmore	Gun Room Steward	Southampton Hants		24
William Fowler	Paym's Bowers Steward	Bristol		26
John Bridgens	Sub Officers Steward	Woolwich Kent		
John Cowie	Stoker	Bermondsey Surry		32
Thomas Plater	Stoker	Westminster Middlesex		
Charles Coombs	A.B	Greenwich Kent		28
George Thompson	A.B	Staines Berks		27
John Hartnell	A.B	Brompton Kent		25
Thomas Hartnell	A.B	Chatham Kent		23
John Stickland	A.B	Portsmouth Hants		24
William Orren	A.B	Chatham Kent		34
William Closson	A.B	Shetland		25
John Morfin	A.B	Gainsboro Lincoln		25
Charles Best	A.B	Fareham Hants		23
Thomas McConvey	A.B	Liverpool Lancashire		24
Henry Lloyd	A.B	Christiansand Norway		26

"TERROR"

Name	Rank			Age
Francis R M Crozier	Captain			
Edward Little	Lieutenant			
George H Hodgson	Lieutenant			
John Irving	Lieutenant			
Thomas Blanky	Ice Master			
John S Peddie	Surgeon			
Frederick J Hornby	Mate			
Robert Thomas	Mate			
Alexander McDonald	Assistant Surgeon			
Gillies A Macbean	Second Master			
Edmund J H Helpman	Clerk in Charge			
John Lane	Boatswain			
Thomas Honey	Carpenter			
James Thompson	Engineer			
Thomas Johnson	Boatswains Mate	Tiverson Carmarthen		
Alexander Wilson	Carpenters Mate	Holy Island Nova Guinea		33
Reuben Male	Captain Forecastle	Westmarsh Kent		27
David McDonald	Quarter Master	Peterhead Scotland		44
John Kenley	Quarter Master	St Monance Fifeshire		44
William Rhodes	Quarter Master	Biedingstart Kent		31
James Elliott	Sailmaker	Wapfield Kent		20
Returned to England Invalided in the Barretto Junior August 1845				
Thomas Darlington	Caulker	Plymouth Devon		
Samuel Honey	Blacksmith	Plymouth Devon		22
John Torrington	Leading Stoker	Manchester		19
Died 1st January 1846				
John Diggle	Ships Cook	Westminster London		36
John Wilson	Captains Coxswain	Potsea Hants		33
Thomas R Farr	Captain Main Top	Deptford Kent		32
Henry Peglar	Captain Fore Top	London		37
William Goddard	Captain Hold	North Yarmouth		39
Robert Thomas Carr	Armourer	London		23
Cornelius Hickey	Caulkers Mate	Limerick		24
Thomas Jopson	Captains Steward	Marylebone Middlesex		21
Thomas Armitage	Gun Room Steward	Chatham Kent		40
Edward Genge	Paymaster Bowers Steward	Gosport Hants		21
William Gibson	Sub Officers Steward	Lewis		22
William Johnson	Stoker	Kirton Lindsay Lincoln		45
Luke Smith	Stoker	London		27
George J Cann	A.B	Battersea Middlesex		23
William Strong	A.B	Portsmouth Hants		
David Sims	A.B	Gateress Essex		24
John Bailey	A.B	Layton Essex		21
William Jerry	A.B	Pimlico Wales		25
Henry Sait	A.B	Bedner Sussex		
Alexander Berry	A.B	South Ferry Fifeshire		32
John Handford	A.B	Sunderland		28
John Bates	A.B	London		24
Samuel Crispe	A.B	Lynn Norfolk		21
Charles Johnson	A.B			

CHAPTER 4

THE MEMBERS OF SIR JOHN FRANKLIN'S *EREBUS* AND *TERROR* EXPEDITION

While the ships were being prepared at Woolwich, and once the expedition's senior officers, John Franklin, Francis Crozier and James Fitzjames, had been appointed, the recruitment of the ships' complement began. The personnel of *Erebus* and *Terror* fulfilled specific roles. The executive commissioned officers – those ranked captain, commander and lieutenant – made calculations and decisions, gave orders and kept records, assisted by the mates.

◄ **4.1 'List of officers, seamen and marines of Her Majesty's Discovery Ships "Erebus" and "Terror" who sailed from England May 1845 in the Expedition under the command of Captain Sir John Franklin Kt KCH**
The list was compiled from official muster tables, after three graves were discovered at Beechey Island in 1851. It includes the names of 133 people but notes that two men had returned to England as invalids (though this figure was in fact four, reducing the complement to 129).

► **4.2 Captain Sir John Franklin**
At 59, Sir John was more than ten years older than the other expedition members, and the image shown here did not flatter him, as he was suffering from influenza when it was taken.

⋀ 4.3 Captain Francis Crozier
As captain of HMS *Terror*, the ship he had commanded during James Ross's Antarctic exploration, Francis Crozier, aged 48, was second-in-command of the expedition. Before that, he had served in three of Parry's Arctic voyages. Crozier had come to know the Franklin family well when the Ross expedition had called at Tasmania while Sir John was governor there.

⋀ 4.4 Commander James Fitzjames
James Fitzjames, aged 31, was Franklin's senior officer in HMS *Erebus*. Although at the outset he might not have thought it relevant to this voyage, he had experience of arduous overland journeys involving hauling equipment, having worked on a scheme to create a steamship route between the Mediterranean and the Indian Ocean via the River Euphrates and the Persian Gulf.

Most of the officers were appointed in early March 1845, two months ahead of the departure date. Six of them – Henry Le Vesconte, James Fairholme, Robert Sargent and Charles Des Voeux of *Erebus*, and George Hodgson and John Irving of *Terror* – came from HMS *Excellent*, the Royal Navy's gunnery training ship at Portsmouth. In a letter home (later published by Benjamin Bell), John Irving explained his reasons for applying: 'It would give me a chance of promotion, on returning after two or three years, and would, at all events, be a change of scene and, if one came back, something to talk of. The *Excellent* is very comfortable; but it is a tiresome kind of life, and Portsmouth is a nasty place. I want something more exciting, and not to be lying in a harbour.' For *Erebus*, Fitzjames gave preference to applicants who had served with him previously – mostly in the Opium Wars in China – whom he knew and trusted.

➤ 4.5 Charles Des Voeux, Mate
Charles Des Voeux was one of the first to be appointed to the expedition, on 4 March 1845, and he was entered in the muster table of HMS *Erebus* on the same day as John Franklin and James Fitzjames. Recruitment continued steadily through March and April, with crew members still joining the ship a week before the expedition's departure in May.

▲ 4.6 Edward Couch, Mate

▲ 4.7 Robert Sargent, Mate

▲ 4.8 Stephen Stanley, Surgeon

▲ 4.9 Lieutenant James Fairholme

▲ 4.10 Lieutenant Henry Le Vesconte

▲ 4.11 Henry Collins, Second Master

As the ships were preparing for departure at Greenhithe on the River Thames, Sir John Franklin's wife Jane arranged for a daguerreotype photographer to visit HMS *Erebus* to capture the images of the officers. Daguerreotypes were a wonderful novelty at the time. Richard Beard had bought the patent covering England from the French inventor of the process, Louis Daguerre, in 1841, and opened the first photographic studios in London. The prices that Beard charged in his studio were one guinea (21 shillings, or £1.05) for a head-and-shoulders portrait and 2 guineas for full length. We do not know whether he charged Lady Franklin more for working on location or less for the bulk order, nor do we know the name of the photographer on the day. Lady Franklin had photographs taken of 14 officers – 13 from *Erebus* and one of Captain Crozier of HMS *Terror*. Commander James Fitzjames had an extra one taken for his family. The exposure time for daguerreotypes varied from a few seconds up to five minutes depending on the light conditions, and the lack of blurring of the subjects suggests that 16 May 1845 was a bright day. The ship was supplied with a camera to take along on the expedition.

An ice master was appointed to each ship to act as a pilot for navigating through the Arctic seas. These were men whose understanding of the way ice moves and whose expertise in choosing the best course to steer a ship through ice fields came from having had careers in the whaling trade, rather than from having served in the Navy. James Reid of Aberdeen, who joined *Erebus*, had worked his way up over more than 30 years to become a well-respected whaling captain. Thomas Blanky of Hull had not only worked in commercial whaling but had been on exploration voyages before. He had been on two of Parry's voyages, serving in HMS *Griper* in 1824 and in HMS *Hecla* in 1827. Blanky had also endured John Ross's near-fatal *Victory* expedition in 1829–33.

➤ **4.12 James Reid, Ice Master**
James Reid was a whaling captain from Aberdeen in his late 40s who had made Arctic voyages since the age of 13. The Admiralty appointed him to this expedition for his expertise in sailing through ice. He wrote to his wife, 'Lady Franklin has ordered all the officers' likenesses to be taken, and mine among the rest, with my uniform on.'

⋀ 4.13 Lieutenant Graham Gore
As mate on Captain George Back's voyage aboard HMS *Terror* in 1836–37, Graham Gore had experienced a perilous winter adrift in pack ice. Since then he had served in the Opium War in China in 1840 and on HMS *Beagle*'s voyage to explore Australia in 1841 and 1842. He was skilled at charting and sketching, and also played the flute.

⋀ 4.14 Charles Osmer, Purser and Paymaster
Charles Osmer had joined the Royal Navy as a clerk in 1819. He had previously seen the Pacific end of the North-West Passage, as he had taken part in Captain Beechey's voyage in HMS *Blossom*, which had been sent to the Bering Strait via Cape Horn in an unsuccessful attempt to join up with John Franklin's second overland expedition in 1827.

◀ **4.15 Portrait of Alexander McDonald**
Dr Alexander McDonald, the assistant surgeon of HMS *Terror* on the Franklin expedition, had graduated from the Royal College of Surgeons of Edinburgh in 1838. Two years later he served on a whaling vessel commanded by Captain William Penny and then wrote a book about the voyage and an Inuk named Eenoolooapik, whom Penny had brought back to Scotland.

The ice masters were certainly not the only men on the expedition with previous polar experience, and they were not the only ones, either, to be undeterred by the danger and ordeals they had been through before. Among the naval officers, as well as Captains Franklin and Crozier, Lieutenant Graham Gore had served on George Back's *Terror* voyage of 1836–37, and Charles Osmer, the purser and paymaster, had been to the Bering Strait with Captain Beechey in HMS *Blossom* in 1825–28.

The purser and the lower-ranked clerk in charge in *Terror* were in accountant roles, responsible for provisions and supplies. Then there were surgeons who, as men of science, were expected to carry out various observations as well as to attend to medical matters. The two surgeons, Stephen Stanley of *Erebus* and John Peddie of *Terror*, were experienced naval officers. Stanley had joined the Navy in 1838 and had served in the same ship as James Fitzjames in the Opium War in 1842. Peddie, the oldest of the medical team at 29, had previously served on at least two naval ships. He was married with a baby daughter when he joined Franklin's expedition. The assistant surgeons of both ships, Alexander McDonald of *Terror* and Harry Goodsir of *Erebus*, had, like John Peddie, trained at the Royal College of Surgeons in Edinburgh. Peddie had graduated in 1836, McDonald in 1838 and Goodsir in 1840. Alexander McDonald, assistant surgeon of *Terror*, had previous Arctic experience: he had been on a whaling voyage to Baffin Bay from Aberdeen in 1840. On that voyage, the captain, William Penny, had been searching the inlets on the west coast of the bay for good whale-hunting areas. A young Inuk named Eenoolooapik went back on the ship to Scotland, and McDonald wrote a book about him and the voyage. Harry Goodsir had not been to sea before, and had left his job as conservator of the museum of the Royal College of Surgeons of Edinburgh to join the expedition for the opportunities it offered to carry out new research in natural history.

The three warrant officers for each ship were the boatswain, the carpenter and the engineer. Together they were responsible for maintaining every aspect of the vessels, with the boatswain concerned principally with the deck and rigging, the carpenter with the hull, spars and boats, and the engineer with the engine and heating system. Below them in rank were the petty officers,

◄ **4.16 Acting Assistant Surgeon Harry Goodsir**
Dr Goodsir had never been to sea before he joined HMS *Erebus* as acting assistant surgeon and expedition naturalist. He had studied medicine at Edinburgh and was conservator of the museum of the Royal College of Surgeons there. When no news was heard of the expedition, his brother Robert went on two of the voyages that set out in search of it, in 1849 and 1850.

some of whom answered to them directly. The boatswain's team included the boatswain's mate and a sailmaker, and the carpenter also had a mate and a caulker. The engineer, a recent rank, did not have a mate, but each ship had a blacksmith and two stokers. Thomas Johnson, who had been a petty officer in *Terror* in the Antarctic, rejoined the ship as boatswain's mate, and Luke Smith, who had been an able seaman on the Antarctic voyage, was now *Terror*'s stoker. Each ship had set out with an armourer, who was a skilled metalworker and gunsmith, but both armourers – Thomas Burt from *Erebus* and Robert Carr from *Terror* – were sent home from Greenland as invalids, along with two other men from *Terror*: sailmaker James Elliot and Royal Marine William Aitken.

Other petty officers were in charge of operating various parts of the ship – namely, the captains of the foretop, the maintop, the forecastle and the hold. Thomas Farr was *Terror*'s captain of the maintop for both the Antarctic and this voyage. Each ship also had three quartermasters, helmsmen at the wheel on the quarterdeck, who were responsible for the steering of the ship. The captains also had coxswains who were in charge of handling their boats. Franklin's coxswain, James Rigden, had been a petty officer in *Erebus* in the Antarctic.

The rest of the petty officers had 'domestic' roles. The ships had one cook each, both of whom had served in *Erebus* in the Antarctic: Richard Wall resumed his post as *Erebus*'s cook, while John Diggle, who was an able seaman on the earlier voyage, became cook of *Terror*.

Stewards were assigned to the captain, the subordinate officers and the purser. There was also a gunroom steward for the Royal Marines. Francis Crozier's steward during the Antarctic voyage, Thomas Jopson, joined him again for this expedition.

The crews mainly consisted of able seamen, with years of skill and experience. Several of the men who signed on as able seamen were promoted in early May to petty officer roles, such as captain of the forecastle, quartermaster and stoker. Promotion did not, however, come to William Jerry, who was ranked able seaman in HMS *Terror* both in the Antarctic and on the Franklin expedition, perhaps because he did not impress the officers or because he did not want the responsibility.

The ships had no ordinary seamen (the rank below able seaman), but each ship had two Boys First Class, aged 18 and 19, as trainees. Each ship also had a contingent of Royal Marines, seven in *Erebus* and six in *Terror*, led by a sergeant and a corporal. The Marine officers answered directly to the ship's captain as one of their roles was to maintain crew discipline. They were also charged with defending the ships and the parties that were sent out from them by manning the guns and firing muskets. Marines could also be expected to help with unskilled heavy work, such as turning capstans to weigh anchor, hauling on ropes, pulling sledges and using ice saws.

The ships' muster books, which recorded when people were appointed and where they had come from, show that perhaps one-sixth of the crew were from northern ports – mostly either from ports in Scotland or from Hull – but the greatest proportion, about one-third, came from the Thames and Medway area, as might be expected of ships based at Woolwich. The other half came from a wide range of places, mostly from coastal areas, such as the naval ports of Plymouth and Portsmouth, but also from inland areas in the case of the engineers and marines.

The Admiralty awarded Arctic expedition members double pay from the date of sailing. Pay was calculated by the lunar month, with 13 lunar months per year. The double rate of pay for able seamen and captain's stewards was £3. 8s. per month; for captains of the forecastle, maintop and hold, it was £4. 10s.; and for caulkers, sailmakers and blacksmiths it was £4.18s. Ship's cooks were paid £5. 6s. Stokers received £4. 12. in summer, but in the winter months, when the engines could not be used, their pay was reduced to able seamen's rates. These wages, although twice what the men were used to, were not astronomically high at a time when a railway navvy might earn £3 per month.

QUEEN'S STORES.—Persons purchasing this Paper are liable to a Prosecution.

No. on the Muster Book	MEN'S NAMES — To follow each other in the order they stand on the Ship's Book	Quality	Rate per Month — Not to be written in	Declaration to whom the Allotment shall be paid — Name	Wife, Father, Mother, or Trustee	Where and when Married; if to a Child, its Name, Age, and where Baptized
51	Jas Elliot	Sailmaker	2 12 0	Emma Amelia Elliott	Sister	
52	Thos Jopson	Capt Stew	1 16	Wm Jopson	Father	
53	Jno Kenley	Qmr	2 4	Helen Kenley	Wife	Jarrow Life Whar 1842
54	Jas Walker	AB	1 16 0	Ann Wood	Sister	
55	Edwd Genge	Sym Steward	2 4 0	Maria Genge	Sister	
56	Willm Rhodes	Qmr	2 8 1	Mary Rhodes	Wife	London 16 Dec 1844
57	Wm Wentyall	AB	1 16	Hannah Wentyall	Wife	London 2 Sept 1836
25	Jno Bates @ Wm	AB	1 16 0	Ann Bates	Mother	—
58	John Torrington	Leading Stoker	2 16	Mary Torrington	Mother	—
3	Jas Thompson	Engineer Mate	13 0 0	Willm Thompson	Father	—
1	Marines 3d Class Willm Hedges	Corporal	1 8 0	Eliza Hedges	Wife	Charlton 8 Feb 1844
	FM Crozier	Captain		Edward Little	Senr Lieutenant	

Crew members and marines were given the option of providing their relations with financial support while they were away, through the 'allotment' system (naval officers were not included, as they were paid via agents). To do this, the men had to provide their relatives' details, which were then entered on the ship's allotment list; they had to state the amount of money they wanted them to be able to withdraw each month and then sign to authorise it. A total of 41 men from *Erebus* and 33 from *Terror* (disregarding those who were sent home) made allotments. The allotment lists provide fascinating information about family life and also give the names and addresses of crew members' next of kin. They reveal another interesting detail about the men of the expedition as well: 18 of them were so illiterate that they were not even able to write their own names, and signed instead with an X.

Twenty men, including some in their thirties, allocated their pay to their mothers. Among them were John Hartnell, who died of disease early in the voyage and was buried at Beechey Island, and his younger brother Thomas. Their mother lived in New Brompton, Kent, close to where they had been born. Five men made allotments to their fathers. The mother of John Diggle, ship's cook, as well as the father of William Gibson, subordinate officers' steward, lived at smart London addresses, suggesting that they were live-in servants. Six men made allotments to their sisters and three to their brothers. Two made allotments to trustees, and one of these was specifically for a child.

Thirty-eight men nominated their wives to receive their pay, which shows that a significant proportion of the members of the expedition were married – nearly a third if John Franklin, Charles Osmer and John Peddie are included in the total. The Admiralty would only make payment to lawfully wedded wives, and the place and date of marriage had to be recorded in the allotment list. James Brown, the caulker, could not remember whether his had taken place in 1837 or 1838. Three weddings had taken place shortly before the expedition departed: James Rigden (Franklin's coxswain) married in March and Daniel Bryant (sergeant of marines) in April. Samuel Brown, boatswain's mate (who had served on Ross's Antarctic voyage under the alias William Hardy, which hints at a complicated life), also married in April. Three others had married in the previous December. It is possible that some men made payments to their relatives that were to be passed on to their unmarried partners.

James Reid, ice master, had been married longer than anyone else. His last letter to his wife, though intended to be reassuring, reveals his underlying anxieties about the possibility of not returning: 'It may be two years – it may be three or four but I am quite willing to go. Sir John told me that if I went the voyage [sic] with him, and landed safely in England again, I would be looked after all my life. Mr Enderby [a whaling company owner] has been a good friend to me. He will look after you if I should never return, but that never comes into my head. A number of people think it strange of me going, but they would go if they knew as much about ice as I know.' He said that he and the other ice master, Thomas Blanky, had insured their lives for £100 each and made the following promise to his wife: 'This voyage will be the last that I will ever make.'

◀ **4.17 A page from the Allotment list of HMS *Terror***
This is part of the 'List of persons belonging to Her Majesty's Ship *Terror* desirous of allotting part of their monthly pay or wages'. John Torrington, the stoker buried at Beechey Island in 1846, is listed towards the bottom of the page as allotting £2 and 16 shillings a month to his mother. The opposite page gives her address in Manchester.

THE MEN OF HMS *EREBUS*

This list is compiled from the Muster tables for *Erebus* (ADM 38/672); and the Allotment lists for *Erebus* (ADM 27/90 pp 321-325) held at The National Archives.

Officers

Sir John Franklin, Captain, Commanding the Expedition

James Fitzjames, Commander

Graham Gore, Lieutenant

Henry T.D. Le Vesconte, Lieutenant

James W. Fairholme, Lieutenant

James Reid, Ice Master
Wife Ann Reid, married in Montrose on 28 September 1818; 21 Prince Regent Street, Aberdeen

Stephen S. Stanley, Surgeon

Harry D.S. Goodsir, Assistant Surgeon

Charles H. Osmer, Paymaster and Purser

Robert O. Sargent, Mate

Charles F. Des Voeux, Mate

Edward Couch, Mate

Henry F. Collins, Second Master

Warrant Officers

Thomas Terry, Boatswain
Wife Sarah Ann Terry, married in Ramsgate 27 July 1842; 3 Hardness Street, Ramsgate

John Weekes, Carpenter
Mother Rachel Weekes, 34 Cumberland Street, Portsea

John Gregory, Engineer
Wife Hannah Gregory, married in Ashton under Lime, Lancashire, in 1822; 7 Ely Place, London

Petty Officers

Samuel Brown (alias William Hardy), Boatswain's Mate, aged 27, born in Hull
Wife Mary Brown, married in St Georges in the Fields Roman Catholic Chapel, 7 April 1845; 40 Artillery Place, Woolwich

Thomas Watson, Carpenter's Mate, aged 40, born in Great Yarmouth, Norfolk
Brother Valentine Watson, Coal Exchange, Broad Street, Point, Portsmouth

Phillip Reddington, Captain of the Forecastle, aged 28, born in Brompton, Kent
Wife Elizabeth Reddington, married in Chatham, December 1844; 28 Manor Street, Brompton

Daniel Arthur, Quartermaster, aged 35, born in Aberdeen
Wife Ann Arthur, married Dundee April 1835; Peter's Court, St Andrew's Place, Dundee

William Bell, Quartermaster, aged 36, born in Dundee
Wife Margaret Bell, married in Dundee in November 1831; William Street, Dundee

John Downing, Quartermaster, aged 34, born in Plymouth, Devon
Sister Elizabeth Blue, Corner of Bath Street, Millbay, Plymouth
Signed X

John Murray, Sailmaker, aged 43, born in Glasgow

James W. Brown, Caulker, aged 28, born in Deptford, Kent
Wife Sophia Brown, married in Bromley in 1837 or 1838; 8 Ann Street, Woolwich
Signed JA X (his mark)

William Smith, Blacksmith, aged 28, born in Thibnam [Tibenham], Norfolk
Wife Rebecca Ann Smith, married in Stepney in 1843; 6 Market Hill, Woolwich
Signed X

James Hart, Leading Stoker, aged 33, born in Hampstead, Middlesex
Trustee William Sharp, 9 Alfred Place, Clapham

Richard Wall, Ship's Cook, aged 45, born in Hull
Wife Hannah Wall, married in Plumstead in 1834; 4 John Street, New Town, Woolwich
Signed X

James Rigden, Captain's Coxswain, aged 32, born in Upper Deal, Kent
Wife Caroline Rigden, married Kingston, Portsea, March 1845; North Road, Landport, Portsea

John Sullivan, Captain of the Maintop, aged 28, born in Gillingham, Kent
Wife Julia Sullivan, married in Gillingham in December 1844; King's Court, Middle Street, Brompton
Signed X

Robert Sinclair, Captain of the Foretop, aged 25, born in Kirkwall, Orkney
Mother Grace Sinclair, Kirkwall

Joseph Andrews, Captain of the Hold, aged 35, born in Edmonton, Middlesex

Francis Dunn, Caulker's Mate, aged 25, born in Llanelli, South Wales
Mother Mary Dunn, Llanelli, South Wales

Edmund Hoar, Captain's Steward, aged 23, born in Portsea, Hants

Richard Aylmore, Gunroom Steward, aged 24, born Southampton, Hampshire
Mother Ann Aylmore, 5 Orchard Place, Limehouse

William Fowler, Paymaster and Purser's
Steward, aged 26, born in Bristol,
Somerset
Father Samuel Fowler,
16 Cumberland Street, Hackney Road

John Bridgens,
Subordinate Officers' Steward,
aged 26, born in Woolwich, Kent
Mother Harriet Richards, 3 New Road,
Woolwich
Signed X

John Cowie, Stoker, aged 32,
born in Bermondsey, Surrey
Wife, Eliza Cowie, married in Rochester,
8 May 1838; Grove Cottage, Chatham

Thomas Plater, Stoker, age not stated,
born in Westminster, Middlesex
Wife Mary Ann Plater, married at
St Andrews, London, 28 Dec 1842, 12
Bedford Street, Liquor Pond Street,
Holborn, London

Able Seamen

Charles Coombs, AB, aged 28,
born in Greenwich, Kent
Trustee for a child,
Rachel Hannah Mears,
5 Bridge Street, Greenwich

George Thompson, AB, age 27,
born in Staines, Berkshire
Brother William Thompson,
Sun Tavern, Mason Street, Lambeth
Signed X

John Hartnell, AB, aged 25,
born in Brompton, Kent
Mother Sarah Hartnell,
New Brompton, Kent
[Died 4th January 1846 and buried
at Beechey Island]

Thomas Hartnell, AB, aged 23,
born in Chatham, Kent
Mother Sarah Hartnell,
New Brompton, Kent

John Stickland, AB, aged 24,
born in Portsmouth, Hampshire
Mother Ann Stickland,
Watt's Place, Chatham

William Orren, AB, aged 34,
born in Chatham, Kent
Mother Margaret Orren,
High Street, Brompton, Kent
Signed X

William Clossan, AB, aged 25,
born in Shetland

John Morfin, AB, aged 25,
born in Gainsborough, Lincolnshire
Brother Thomas Morfin, 19 New Road,
Deptford
Signed X

Boys

George Chambers, aged 18,
born in Woolwich, Kent

David Young, aged 18,
born in Sheerness, Kent

Royal Marines

Daniel Bryant, Sergeant, aged 31,
born in Shepton Montague, Somerset
Wife Mary Ann Bryant, married in
Rotherhithe April 1845; 47 Lower
Park Street, Greenwich

Alexander Paterson, Corporal,
aged 30, born in Inverness

Robert Hopcraft, Private, aged 38,
born in Nottingham

William Pilkington, Private, aged 28,
born in Kilrush, Co. Clare

William Braine, Private, aged 31,
born in Oakhill, Somerset
[Died 3rd April 1846 and buried
at Beechey Island]

Joseph Healey, Private, aged 29,
born in Manchester
Mother Karan Healey,
31 Buckley Street, Manchester
Signed X

William Reed, Private, aged 28,
born in Bristol

THE MEN OF HMS *TERROR*

This list is compiled from the Muster tables for *Terror* (ADM 38/1962); and the Allotment lists for *Terror* (ADM 27/90 pp 316-320) held at The National Archives.

Officers

Francis R.M. Crozier, Captain

Edward Little, Lieutenant

George H. Hodgson, Lieutenant

John Irving, Lieutenant

Thomas Blanky, Ice Master
Wife, Esther Blanky, married in Whitby, 2 January 1835; 41 Grafton Street, Torbath Park, Liverpool

John S. Peddie, Surgeon

Alexander McDonald, Assistant Surgeon

Edwin J. Helpman, Clerk in Charge

Frederick J. Hornby, Mate

Robert Thomas, Mate

Gillies A. MacBean, Second Master

Warrant Officers

John Lane, Boatswain
Wife, Eliza Lane, married in Portsmouth, 10 July 1838; 6 King Street, Church Path, Kingston, Portsea

Thomas Honey, Carpenter
Wife, Margaret Honey, married in Plymouth, 1840?; 51 Duke Street, Devonport

James Thompson, Engineer
Father, William Thompson, Meadow Lane, Leeds

Petty Officers

Thomas Johnson, Boatswain's Mate, aged 28, born in Wisbech, Cambridge
Sister, Jane Johnson, 4 Branson's Court, Heath Street, Hampstead

Alexander Wilson, Carpenter's Mate, aged 27, born in Holy Island, North Durham
Wife, Sarah Wilson, married 24 June 1839, Bishop Wearmouth, Durham; 21 St Ann's Street, Limehouse, London

Reuben Male, Captain of the Forecastle, aged 27, born in Woolwich, Kent
Mother, Hannah Male, 3 Church Street, Deptford

David McDonald, Quartermaster, aged 46, born in Peterhead, Scotland
Wife, Ann McDonald, married in Peterhead 28 September 1828; 5 Errol Street, Peterhead

John Kenley, Quartermaster, aged 44, born in St Monans, Fifeshire
Wife, Helen Kenley, married in Forgue, Fife, 4 November 1822; 60 Blackscroft, Butchersland, Dundee

William Rhodes, Quartermaster, aged 31, born in Redingstreet, Kent
Wife, Mary Rhodes, married in London, 16 December 1844; 2 Upper Harley Street, Cavendish Square, London

Thomas Darlington, Caulker, aged 29, born in Plymouth, Devon
Wife, Sarah Darlington, married Plymouth 27 Aug 1837;
28 Broomfield Place, Deptford – moved to 104 Union Street, Stonehouse (Plymouth) 4 July 1845

Samuel Honey, Blacksmith, aged 22, born in Plymouth, Devon

John Torrington, Leading Stoker, aged 19, born in Manchester
Mother, Mary Torrington, 4 Grey's Buildings, Oxford Street, Manchester. Struck out and replaced with 33 Little James Street, Oxford Street, Manchester

John Diggle, Ships Cook, aged 36, born in Westminster, London
Mother, Phoebe Diggle, 13 Dacres Street, Westminster

John Wilson, Captain's Coxswain, aged 33, born in Portsea, Hants
Wife, Jane Wilson, married Portsmouth 1st September 1837; 15 Briton Street, St Georges Square, Portsea

Thomas R. Farr, Captain of the Maintop, aged 32, born in Deptford, Kent
Sister, Louisa Hardy, 3 Orchard Hill, Lime Kiln, Greenwich
Signed X

Harry Peglar, Captain of the Foretop, aged 37, born in London

William Goddard, Captain of the Hold, aged 39, born in Yarmouth, Norfolk

Cornelius Hickey, Caulker's Mate, aged 24, born in Limerick

Thomas Jopson, Captain's Steward, aged 27, born in Marylebone, Middlesex
Father, William Jopson, 3 Gee Street, Brick Lane, London

Thomas Armitage, Gun-room Steward, aged 40, born in Chatham, Kent
Wife, Cecilia Armitage, married in Gillingham, 2 October 1826; 3 New Road, Chatham
Signed X

Edward Genge, Paymaster & Purser's Steward, aged 21, born in Gosport, Hants
Sister, Maria Genge, Cold Harbour, Gosport

William Gibson, Subordinate Officers' Steward, aged 22, born in London
Father, Stewart Gibson, 23 Upper Ogle Street, St Marylebone, London

William Johnson, Stoker, aged 45, born in Kirton Lindsey, Lincoln
Wife Ann Johnson, married Hull 26 March 1826; Whips Court, Hull, moved to 53 Upper Cornwall Street, St Georges in the East, 28 Sept 1852 [Shadwell]
Signed X

Luke Smith, Stoker, aged 27, born in London

Able Seamen

George J. Cann, aged 23, born in Battersea, Middlesex
Mother, Margaret Cann, 44 Blackman Street, Southwark

William Strong, aged 22, born in Portsmouth, Hants
Mother, Hannah Strong, Green Lane, Hambledon, Hants

David Sims, aged 24, born in Gedney, Lincoln

John Bailey, aged 21, born in Leyton, Essex

William Jerry, aged 29, born in Pembroke, Wales

Henry Sait, aged 23, born in Bognor, Sussex
Mother, Catharine Whittington, West Street, Bognor
Signed X

Alexander Berry, aged 32, born in South Ferry, Fifeshire
Wife, Eleanor Berry, married in South Shields, 19 February 1839; Thames Street, South Shields

John Handford, aged 28, born in Sunderland
Mother, Ann Handford, Mill Hill, Sunderland

John Bates, aged 24, born in London
Mother, Ann Bates, Spring Cottage, Chalk Road, Redington
Signed X

Samuel Crispe, aged 24, born in Lynn, Norfolk
Wife, Mary Ann Crispe, married in Gillingham, 5th April 1843; 4 Cross Street on the Brook, Chatham

Charles Johnson, aged 28, born in Halifax, Nova Scotia

William Shanks, aged 29, born in Dundee, Scotland
Wife, Antasker Shanks, married in Dundee, 16 May 1827, Fish Street, Dundee

David Leys, aged 37, born in Montrose, Scotland
Wife, Christina Leys, married in Braichan [Brechin?], nr Aberdeen, 27 Nov 1827; 9 Trinity Key [sic], Aberdeen

William Sinclair, aged 30, born in Sallaway [Sallachy?], Scotland

Edwin Lawrence, aged 30, born in London
Wife, Harriet Lawrence, married in London, 25 August 1838, 3 Spencers Street, St George in the East, London

Magnus Manson, aged 28, born in Shetland

James Walker, aged 29, born in South Shields
Sister, Ann Wood, Hugh Street, South Shields

William Wentzall, aged 33, born in London
Wife, Hannah Wentzall, married in London, 2 September 1836; 14 Little Thames Street, Greenwich

George Kinnaird, aged 23, born in Hastings, Sussex

Boys

Robert Golding, aged 19, born in Deptford, Kent

Thomas Evans, aged 18, born in Deptford, Kent

Royal Marines

Solomon Tozer, Sergeant, aged 34, born in Axbridge, Somerset

William Hedges, Corporal, aged 30, born in Bradford, Wilts
Wife, Eliza Hedges, married in Charlton, 8 April 1844; 10 Godfrey Street, Woolwich

William Heather, Private, aged 37, born in Battersea, Surrey

Henry Wilkes, Private, aged 28, born in Leicester

John Hammond, Private, aged 32, born in Bradford, Yorkshire

James Daly, Private, aged 30, born in [Tubberclare?]

➤ **5.1 *HMS* Erebus *in the Ice***
François-Etienne Musin, 1846

CHAPTER 5

EXPEDITION LIFE

For the first few weeks of the *Erebus* and *Terror* expedition, until it left Greenland in July 1845, the letters the men sent home give some idea of what life was like on board. For the rest of the voyage we must rely on inference from the physical conditions, on what we know about naval custom, and on the experience of other Arctic expeditions.

Life on board *Erebus* and *Terror* was very cramped. The only inside spaces were the lower deck, which was used for accommodation, and the orlop deck and hold, which were used for storage. Everybody lived literally at close quarters with each other, in a space a little longer but

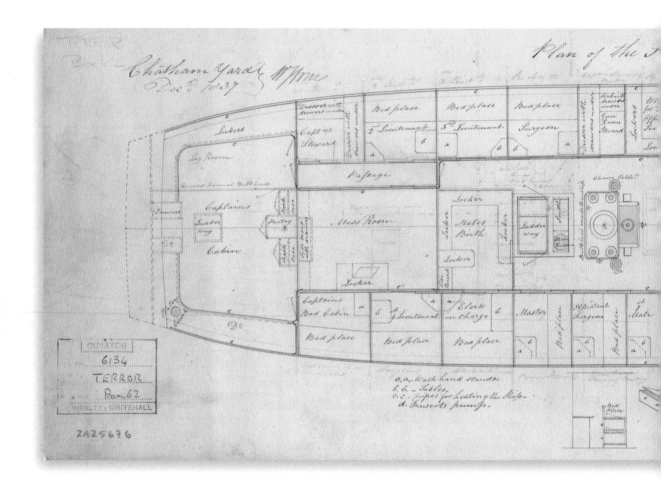

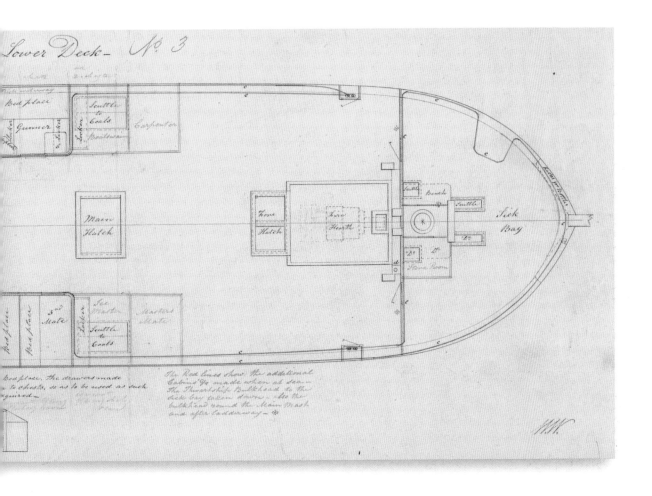

▲ 5.2 Plan of HMS *Terror*'s lower deck

The only inside spaces in *Erebus* and *Terror* were the lower deck, which was used for accommodation, and the orlop deck and hold, which were used for storage. This plan was drawn in preparation for the earlier voyage to the Antarctic. Both ships shared a very similar layout. The tightness of these spaces would increase the difficulty of investigating the wrecks of the ships underwater.

narrower than a 25-metre swimming pool. The Admiralty had not stinted on the manning of the ships, perhaps assuming that the greater the manpower, the greater the chance of success. Captain Crozier, who commanded *Terror*, wrote to John Henderson, an old messmate from one of Parry's voyages, that he was glad that he had reduced his complement from 68 to 62, though he thought it was still too many, recollecting that in *Fury* they had only 58 or 60.

Humans were not the only living things on board. The ships started out with cattle, sheep, pigs and hens to be eaten during the early stages of the voyage, and they also took pets. *Erebus* had three: a monkey that Lady Franklin had presented to the ship, an old Newfoundland dog named Neptune and a cat. In a letter to his father, Lieutenant Fairholme said that old Neptune had lost much of his unwieldiness so that he could now run up and down steep steps with ease, and he was very popular. The monkey was an annoying thief, but he was so amusing that no one wanted to hurt him.

The cat would be needed to catch rats, which could be a problem even in the Arctic. They would probably have come on board at the dockyards and were almost impossible to eradicate. In 1986, when scientists examined the frozen body of William Braine, a Royal Marine from HMS *Erebus* who was one of the three men who had died in 1846, they found teeth marks in his flesh. They concluded that rats had attacked his body before its burial.

The layout of the accommodation in the ships mirrored the hierarchy and work groupings on board. The captain's cabin was at the stern, and it was the operations room of the ship. It was the best-lit interior space, making it ideal for poring over charts spread out on a table. The cabin was also used for the captain to meet and occasionally dine with his officers, and he had a separate sleeping cabin next to it. When the engine was running, the vibration in the cabin must have been tremendous. Naval captains were supposed to keep themselves at a distance from their officers for most of the time so that overfamiliarity did not undermine discipline. Crozier wrote to Henderson that he disliked living alone but knew it could not be otherwise. Captain Franklin had a very different style of command. Edward Couch, one of *Erebus*'s mates, wrote approvingly in one of his letters home that Franklin entertained three officers at dinner with him every day, including those of HMS *Terror* when the weather permitted, and that he had brought along enough wine for four people every day and for a full cabin twice a week for three years.

The mess room for the senior officers was forward of the captain's cabin, and that of the junior officers was still further forward. The sleeping cabins were ranged against the sides of the ships and equipped with space-saving furniture designed by the shipwrights at Chatham. There were drawers under the bed places and seats and lockers above. The cabins followed the same progression from high to lower status, with the lieutenants, the surgeons and the purser taking precedence over the masters and mates. Then came the stewards and the boatswain, carpenter and engineer. Because one of the roles of the marines was to protect the ship's officers from the crew, their living space was in between and they ate their meals separately.

The crew did not have fixed bed places – or any privacy – but slung their hammocks from the deck beams in the open area forward of the mainmast. Their work was organised on a watch system, with only half of the crew resting at any time, so this helped to reduce the crowding. Money for bedding was deducted from their six months' advance pay. To eat their meals, the men sat on their sea chests at mess tables fixed to the sides of the ship, conveniently close to the galley. The warmth from the galley stove was welcome, but food preparation involved a lot of boiling and the space was always damp.

Provisions were supplied by the official Royal Navy victuallers, and the decisions about the type and quantity of food needed to keep the expedition members healthy for three years were

⋀ 5.3 Food tin, 1845
The soup tins were made of tin-plated iron sheet metal, sealed with solder. This example still retains some red paint and part of the label with instructions for preparing the contents. At this time specialist tin-opening tools had not been invented, and a hammer and chisel appear to have been used to cut a hole in the lid.

◀ **5.4 Sir John Franklin's fork and spoon**
George Adams, 1844–45
The expedition officers engraved their silver cutlery with their crests or initials. Franklin's crest was a conger eel's head between two branches. The silver hallmark shows that these items were made in 1844–45, so Franklin bought them especially for this voyage. In contrast, Lieutenant Robert Sargent took some old family silver with him, hallmarked 1792.

based on the experience of previous polar voyages. There was only one cook allocated to each ship. Once the livestock carried on deck had all been slaughtered and eaten, protein in the diet consisted of salt beef and salt pork as well as canned meat and soup, with a large quantity of tinned food included in the ships' provisions. Food canning was a relatively recent invention, but it had been in use for a number of years prior to the expedition and had proved to be a satisfactory means of preserving food. For example, James Ross's Antarctic expedition had relied on tinned provisions without any ill effects. However, there has been speculation that the tins manufactured by Stephen Goldner that were supplied to the Franklin expedition may have caused lead poisoning and botulism.

Canned or salted food could be supplemented by freshly caught fish, birds, deer and even polar bears, which Arctic explorers reported as tasting rather like beef. The meat would have been accompanied by hard-baked ship's biscuit (called 'bread'), dried peas and preserved vegetables, including potatoes and carrots. There was also concentrated 'portable soup' (in dried cakes) and barley. Puddings could be made from sugar, oatmeal, suet, currants and chocolate, and there was tea to drink, as well as a daily ration of a quarter of a pint of rum, issued watered-down as 'grog'. Lemon juice, cranberries, pickled onions, cabbage and walnuts were taken to ward off scurvy.

Stewards served meals to the officers, who dined in a more formal way than the men. The expedition officers had to provide their own silver cutlery. James Reid, the ice master of *Erebus*, complained to his wife about the expense of having to buy himself silver forks and spoons to use. The officers also provided themselves with alcoholic drinks and other luxuries to cheer up their diet.

A total of 7,088 pounds of tobacco was supplied to the ships. This was either chewed or smoked in pipes, as cigarettes had not yet been adopted in Britain, though officers smoked cigars. Franklin himself had used snuff for most of his life, but the doctor who treated him for influenza shortly before his departure advised him to give it up, so Franklin resolved to use smelling salts instead. The quantity of tobacco taken on the voyage was almost double that of soap, which may give an idea of the atmosphere below deck, although everybody was required to wash themselves and their underclothes regularly. Time was allocated during the week to tasks such as washing and mending clothes.

Warm clothing was supplied for the crew, while the officers had to provide their own. The items taken were probably very similar to those taken on George Bass's *Terror* voyage: sea boots, cloth boots with cork soles, various warm jackets, wool-lined weatherproof trousers, wool shirts, swanskin drawers (actually made of a soft woollen fabric), 'comfortables' (scarves or quilts), Welsh wigs (woollen caps with long necks), fur caps and bearskin blankets.

Sewing was a necessary skill for seamen as they had to be able to repair their own clothes, while the stewards had the officers' uniforms to look after. Decorative embroidery and other sailors' crafts helped to pass the time in winter. Commander Fitzjames wrote home that some of *Erebus*'s men had made clothes for the ship's pet monkey.

The main part of the work, of course, consisted of sailing the ships, which were three-masted and rigged with eight sails. When they were sailing through ice fields, the ice master would be up in the crow's nest at the top of the mainmast looking for 'leads' – breaks in the ice that joined up to form channels. The quartermasters, at the ship's wheel, were in charge of steering. Officers calculated the position of the ship and logged progress, weather conditions and occurrences. Ten chronometers (highly accurate watches) were carried on each ship for finding longitude (the ships' east–west position), and these had to be wound and their times compared with each other. Lieutenant Irving was responsible for this task in HMS *Terror*.

The expedition's discoveries were to be surveyed and charted. For this purpose, surveying instruments were used to take bearings on features on the coastline from fixed points, and the depth of the water was measured with sounding lines. This numerical information was recorded in survey books and then plotted out in chart form, drawing lines to connect the surveyed points. It was usual to sketch views of the coast as these coastal profiles would help future navigators recognise where they were.

The officers were also tasked with carrying out additional scientific observations to contribute to biology, geology, meteorology and especially the study of terrestrial magnetism. Terrestrial magnetism was not merely an interesting scientific phenomenon – the ability to predict the relationship between magnetic north

➤ **5.5 Tobacco pipes**
At the time of the expedition, the usual way of smoking tobacco was in clay pipes, but they were quite fragile and if their stems broke they were simply tossed away. The fragments shown here were found at Cape Felix at the north of King William Island, where members of the Franklin expedition set up an observatory to take readings of terrestrial magnetism.

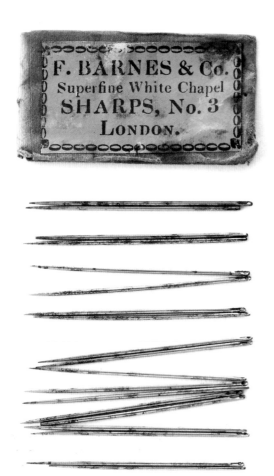

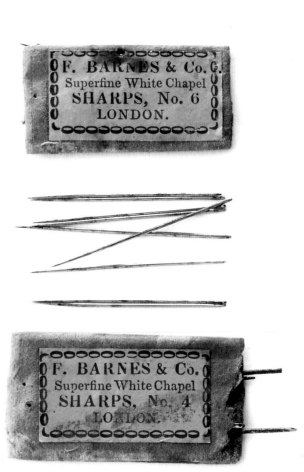

and true north was of vital importance for safety at sea. Ships' compasses show magnetic north, but this constantly varies because the Earth's magnetic field is not regular or static and the magnetic pole itself moves about quite rapidly. Navigators needed to know how to correct their compass readings to true north in order to find their courses on charts.

This observation work had already begun when the expedition was still on the coast of Greenland, as Commander Fitzjames reported in a letter written home from HMS *Erebus* in June 1845. He and Lieutenant Fairholme had been taking magnetic readings in a little square wooden house, while being bitten by large mosquitoes. Despite the insects, Fitzjames gave a very cheerful assessment of the voyage so far and of his shipmates. He said that Dr Harry Goodsir,

F. BARNES & Co.
Superfine White Chapel
SHARPS, No. 1
LONDON

◄ **5.6 Packets of needles**
F Barnes & Co, pre-1845
Packets of needles found by Lieutenant WR Hobson at the
abandoned camp site at Cape Felix on King William Island
in May 1859. Extra supplies of needles were taken on the
expedition as gifts for Inuit.

the expedition's naturalist and acting assistant
surgeon, 'is enthusiastic about all 'ologies …
catches phenomena in a bucket, looks at the
thermometer and every other meter'. The officers
helped him fish up strange animals in nets and
dredges, catching a quantity of cod in the process.

The main job of the surgeons was of course
to look after the health of the crew. They
recommended that some of the men be sent

home from Greenland on medical grounds, but
others who remained on the expedition were
also carrying diseases, including tuberculosis,
which was endemic in Victorian Britain. Despite
the surgeons' efforts, three men died early in
1846 and were buried at Beechey Island. Their
frozen bodies were disinterred in the 1980s and
it was discovered that they had tuberculosis and
died of pneumonia. A further discovery was that
a surgeon had carried out an autopsy on one

◀ **5.7 Dip circle**
Robinson, *c.*1840
Dip circles were used to measure the angle of the Earth's magnetic field. The instrument consists of an iron needle pivoted within a circular brass ring, mounted on a tripod base with screw feet for making it level. Close to the magnetic pole, the tilt of the needle is more vertical than it is further away. The one shown here was found with abandoned bulky equipment on King William Island.

of the men, John Hartnell of HMS *Erebus*, soon after his death. An incision had been made in his chest and abdomen to remove the heart, lungs and liver for examination. They were replaced before the body was sewn up. We cannot know which surgeon did this or why, but Harry Goodsir had a strong interest in pathology, and he seems a likely candidate.

Religion played a major part in the routine of the ship. Sunday was as far as possible a rest day, with services held in the morning and in the evening so that the men of both watches could attend. John Franklin was deeply religious, and Commander Fitzjames noted that he led the prayers with great sincerity, gaining the full attention of the crew. Edward Couch said that Franklin used sermon books but added a great deal himself.

The expedition was expected to spend at least one winter in the ice. Each year in September, the sea froze, and by the end of October the sun dropped below the horizon and would not reappear for three months – and who knew how much longer after that it would be before the sea thawed, if at all? The intention was to anchor the ships in a secure natural harbour before winter set in, where they would be protected from the destructive power of moving ice. The topmasts would then be taken down and sloping canvas roofs would be constructed over the upper decks to throw off the snow. Walls of ice that built up around the ships would provide insulation. Inside, the ships were heated by stoves and heating pipes and lit by candles – 2,700 pounds of candles had been loaded. In midwinter the temperature outside would fall below minus 40 degrees (the point where the Centigrade and Fahrenheit tables converge) and the mercury in thermometers would solidify. Although there was no sun, the sky was starlit and not completely dark, except during thick cloud and snowy weather and at new moon. Sometimes there would be brilliant auroras and other atmospheric effects such as haloes around the moon.

The importance of daily exercise throughout the long, dark winter had long been recognised. In the 1820s Captain Parry had taken a patent barrel organ with bells, drum and triangle on his Arctic voyages, and when the weather was too bad for exercise ashore, he had made his men run round and round the deck, keeping step to a tune on the organ. He said they 'made it the occasion of much humour and frolic among themselves'. Inspired by this, the officers

➤ **5.8 Bomb vessels prepared for the winter: engraving from Parry's *Journal of a voyage for the discovery of a North-West Passage from the Atlantic to the Pacific***

This image of Parry's two bomb vessels, *Hecla* and *Griper*, overwintering in 1819–20, suggests how *Erebus* and *Terror* would have looked during the winter when they were in harbour at Beechey Island. The ships' topmasts have been taken down and their decks are roofed over with timber and canvas awnings. Winters spent trapped in a moving ice field, however, would have been much more precarious.

of *Erebus* and *Terror* bought a barrel organ with a 'playlist' of 50 tunes for each ship.

The winter was also seen as an opportunity to improve the crew's literacy and numeracy. Seventy slates, slate pencils, 200 pens, ink, paper and arithmetic books were taken along for schoolwork, and plenty of books, many of a religious nature, were also provided. The officer's mess had a very extensive library. On Parry's expeditions, handwritten weekly newspapers with humorous content were produced 'to relieve monotony and to promote fun and good fellowship'. The mysterious pieces of writing (sometimes referred to as the 'Peglar papers') which were found near the skeleton of one of Franklin's men who died after the ships were abandoned may have been composed for this purpose. They include doggerel verses, a parody of a popular song and accounts of experiences in Venezuela.

As well as informal music and singing, organised entertainments were held on board Arctic exploration ships, including performances of plays to which the officers and men of the

▲ **5.9 Captain Parry's violin**
GH Hicks, *c*.1819–27
Parry played the violin, and the one shown here is the instrument that he took on his Arctic voyages. He had been the first British naval officer to plan to spend winters in the Arctic, devising a programme of exercise, education and entertainment to maintain health and morale. Franklin's expedition intended to follow his example, but the third winter must have felt interminable.

accompanying ships were invited. Preparations for these involved a large group of people, tasked with constructing and painting sets, making costumes and performing. The entertainments probably went down well during the first two winters, but maintaining morale in the final winter of the expedition (1847–48), when the men were anxious about whether they could reach safety before the provisions ran out, must have been far more difficult.

With the return of daylight in the spring of each year there were more opportunities for hunting game, and preparations would be made then for sledge journeys. Sledging expeditions were able to carry out reconnaissance and surveying over the ice before it thawed sufficiently to allow the ships to break out. Teams of usually six or seven men, led by an officer, man-hauled sledges carrying tents, bedding and supplies that included pemmican (slabs of dried meat and fat). By the early summer of 1848, when the ships were abandoned, the sledge teams of *Erebus* and *Terror* would have reached such a high standard of proficiency that a long overland journey to safety would not have seemed impossible.

➤ **5.10 Shotgun, *c*.1840–44**
Officers brought their own shotguns for shooting game and specimens of Arctic wildlife. The Royal Marines were equipped with muskets, primarily to defend the ship, but their shooting skills would also have been relied on for procuring fresh meat. This shotgun is one of a pair found with the body of an officer in a boat on King William Island.

MIDDLEWEEK   FIRMAN

ROCK

G. F. Mc D.

◄ 5.11 Arctic theatre performance of the play *Charles XII*. From a facsimile of the *Illustrated Arctic News*, published on board HMS *Resolute*, Capt Horatio T Austin, CB, in search of the expedition under Sir John Franklin, by Sherard Osborn

Arctic expeditions from Captain Parry's voyages onwards included theatrical performances among their winter entertainments. Dressing up in women's costumes caused hilarity. This performance of an old Drury Lane hit was put on in 1851 by the officers of HMS *Assistance* during one of the expeditions which went in search of *Erebus* and *Terror*, and the sketch was drawn for the ship's newspaper.

CHAPTER 6

SEARCHING FOR FRANKLIN

◄ 6.1 *HMS* Assistance *and* Pioneer *breaking out of winter quarters, 1854* Captain Walter William May; T.G. Dutton (engraver)

Erebus and *Terror* were last seen by whalers in Baffin Bay in August 1845. They were loaded with provisions for three years and Sir John Franklin expected that it would take at least two summers to complete the North-West Passage. When in January 1847 John Ross offered his services to the Admiralty to lead a search, saying that he had promised Franklin he would do so, the official response was that the Admiralty had 'unlimited confidence in the skills and resources of Sir John Franklin' and there was no need to be anxious about the success of the expedition. It did, however, offer a reward to whalers if they could provide information about the progress of the expedition through Lancaster Sound.

Valley of the glaciers, Greenland

▲ 6.2 *Valley of the glaciers, Greenland.*
***The* Enterprise *and the* Investigator**
WH Browne, 1848
This view of Greenland was sketched by Lieutenant William
Browne of HMS *Enterprise* at the beginning of James Ross's
expedition of 1848–49 in search of Franklin. The Arctic ice did
not melt very much that year and the ships were unable to
make as much progress as had been hoped.

The first to take action was John Richardson,
Franklin's old friend from his overland journeys.
In 1847, knowing that the *Erebus* and *Terror*
expedition was due to run out of food in the
summer of 1848, he began planning an overland
journey to the sea between the Coppermine
and Mackenzie rivers, in case Franklin's ships
had made their way down to the coast of
North America. He joined forces with another
doctor, John Rae, who was an employee of the
Hudson's Bay Company, and in a journey much
better manned and supplied than those he had
undertaken with Franklin, they descended
the Mackenzie to Coronation Gulf in 1848.
They found no trace of *Erebus* and *Terror*, and
although Rae continued the search in 1849, there
was nothing to be seen of the expedition.

Meanwhile, when no news of Franklin had been heard by the autumn of 1847, the Admiralty decided that it did need to prepare to send out search expeditions if they were to reach *Erebus* and *Terror* before their provisions ran out. Captain Moore in HMS *Plover*, along with Captain Kellett in HMS *Herald*, sailed in January 1848 to the Bering Strait to find out whether Franklin's expedition had nearly completed the North-West Passage but had become caught up somewhere near the western exit. In case Franklin had not progressed as far as that, Captain James Ross in HMS *Enterprise* together with Captain Bird in HMS *Investigator* set out in June 1848 to enter Lancaster Sound from the east, as Franklin had done, and attempted to follow his tracks.

Those at home had to wait a long time to find out how the search expeditions got on. Jane Franklin believed passionately that more should be done to rescue her husband's party. She wrote to the President of the United States and to the Czar of Russia to try to involve their countries in the effort. Finding that the whalers were reluctant to spend valuable time searching, she offered a much larger reward from her own funds and planned to buy a ship and commission her own expedition.

In October 1849 the captain of a whale ship came back to Britain with a third-hand Inuit account of four ships frozen in channels leading south from Lancaster Sound. These were taken to be Franklin's and Ross's expeditions, but when

James Ross brought *Enterprise* and *Investigator* back to England very soon afterwards, the account was dismissed as made up. Ross's ships had not been able to penetrate very far at all through Lancaster Sound. Critics of Ross accused him of spending his time in a safe harbour and of sending sledge expeditions in the wrong direction, towards the north magnetic pole instead of towards Cape Walker. (With hindsight, it is now known that the direction in which Ross sent the sledges was correct, but they did not travel far enough to reach King William Island, where the surviving members of the *Erebus* and *Terror* expedition had come ashore after abandoning their ships more than a year earlier.)

In 1850 the Admiralty again sent out searches to both ends of the North-West Passage. Captains McClure and Collinson took HMS *Investigator* and HMS *Enterprise* to the Bering Strait to join *Plover* and *Herald*. Captain Austin in HMS *Resolute* commanded a squadron of four naval vessels that was sent to Lancaster Sound. His second-in-command was Captain Erasmus Ommanney in HMS *Assistance*, and they were each accompanied by a steam vessel (*Intrepid* and *Pioneer*) to tow them if wind or ice conditions were unfavourable. It still seemed possible that members of Franklin's expedition were alive, although they would by now have spent five winters in the ice. John Ross's *Victory* expedition had survived four winters, after all, and nobody doubted the resourcefulness of Franklin and his officers. The searching ships were equipped with balloons, together with apparatus to make gas for them. The balloons were to fly across the Arctic, periodically dropping messages printed on silk that would tell Franklin's expedition where the rescue ships were.

➤ **6.3 Staffordshire pottery figures of Sir John and Lady Franklin, *c.*1850**
When her husband's ships failed to return as planned, Jane, Lady Franklin worked passionately to persuade the government to organise rescue operations. She also offered rewards to whalers and sent out ships at her own expense to extend the coverage of the search. Her devotion to the cause was celebrated at the time in songs and by the production of these pottery figurines.

◄ 6.4 *Snowy Sound, Straits of Magellan.*
Gorgon, Enterprise *and* Investigator
Captain Cowper Phipps Coles, 1850
This sketch shows HMS *Enterprise*
(Captain Collinson) and HMS *Investigator*
(Captain McClure) on the 1850 search
mission, being towed by a steamer through
the Straits of Magellan on their way to
the Bering Strait at the west end of the
North-West Passage. The two ships parted
company in the Pacific Ocean and entered
the Arctic separately.

Despatched by a Balloon from H. M. S. in Lat. N., Long. W. To Sir John Franklin.

▲ 6.5 Balloon message

The balloons dropped pieces of silk bearing messages addressed to Sir John Franklin. They were partly printed but needed to be filled in with important information, including the date and the name of the searching ship and its position, before they were dispatched. Once the messages were dropped, the searchers would then hope to hear a gun being fired or see a smoke signal in response.

◄ 6.6 Arctic balloon, 1852–53

To aid the search for Franklin, George Shepherd invented balloons for distributing messages. The balloons were made of thin paper in a silk net, coloured with red stripes to make them conspicuous. They were filled with hydrogen gas, prepared using a series of casks and tubes. Messages were released when a slow fuse attaching them to the balloon burnt through.

Lady Franklin had succeeded in persuading the Admiralty to pay for two rescue ships (*Lady Franklin* and *Sophia*) to sail under the command of a whaling captain, William Penny. At the same time, John Ross, despite being 72 by now, went on his own expedition, partly funded by public subscription, on board the *Felix*. The ships all congregated at the entrance to Wellington Channel. At Cape Riley and Beechey Island about 230 miles west of the entrance into Lancaster Sound from Baffin Bay, they found the first traces of the missing expedition: the remains of *Erebus* and *Terror*'s 1845–46 winter quarters and the graves of three of Franklin's expedition members, who had died early in 1846.

▲ **6.7 Sketch of *Erebus* and *Terror*'s crews playing cricket**

Captain Austin's search expedition set out in 1850 with some optimism about being able to rescue the missing men. This sketch, kept by Edward Harrison, clerk in charge of HMS *Assistance*, shows one of Franklin's ships perched above an ice field where men are playing cricket near a settlement of igloos labelled 'Erebus', 'Terror' and 'Franklin'. Balloons are dropping messages, while Franklin's lookout, up a flagstaff, waves to a rescue ship.

**⋏ 6.8 The graves of John Torrington, John Hartnell
and William Braine at Beechey Island**
GF McDougall
The first traces of the missing expedition were found
in August 1850 when searchers discovered remains of
its winter quarters at Cape Riley and Beechey Island.
George McDougall, Second Master of HMS *Resolute*,
drew this sketch of the graves of three men who had
died in early 1846.

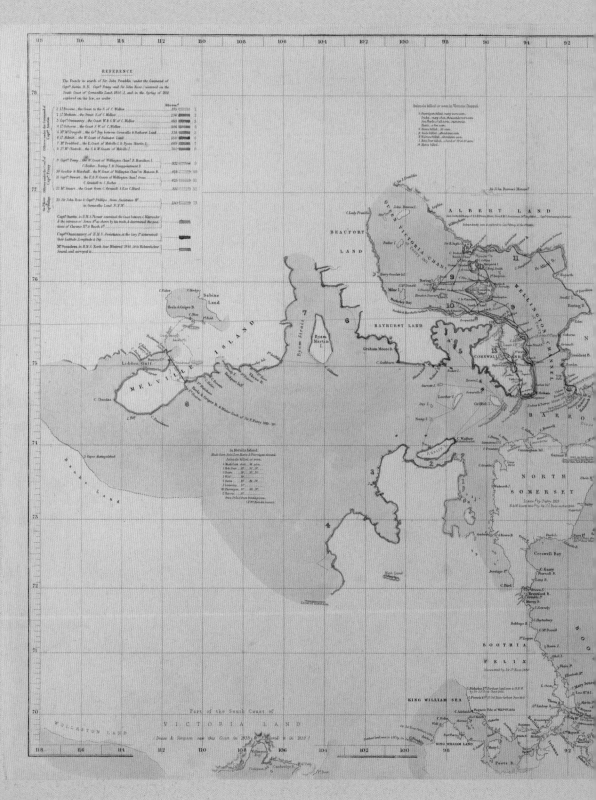

▲ 6.9 Plan of Erebus and Terror Bay: the winter quarters of Sir John Franklin

Drawn from official documents by John Arrowsmith, 1850–51. This plan shows the natural harbour behind Beechey Island where *Erebus* and *Terror* spent the first winter of the expedition, in 1845–46. The location of the graves of John Torrington, William Braine and John Hartnell is marked, along with other features, such as a forge, a wash house and a garden.

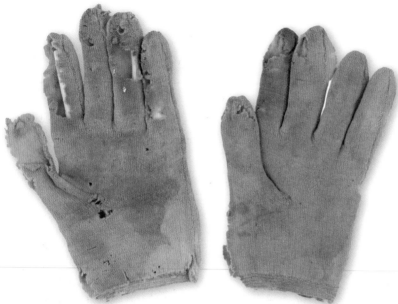

◄ **6.10 Gloves found at Beechey Island**
These gloves belonged to a member of Sir John Franklin's expedition. They are made of knitted cotton and both have a small heart motif in the centre of the palm. They are both for the left hand and may have been worn one inside the other.

➤ **6.11 Dish found at Beechey Island**
This earthenware dish is small enough to fit into a pocket and is decorated with a bird design. What it was used for and why it was left at Beechey Island remain a mystery.

Scrap of Sail Cloth,
from a piece marked —
—"Terror" — found at 38
Cape Riley — the Winter
Quarters of Sir John Franklin

▲ **6.12 Canvas from HMS *Terror***
William Penny found a piece of sailcloth,
marked 'Terror', at Cape Riley in 1850.
This fragment was exhibited at the Naval
Museum in Greenwich after his return.

▲ 6.13 *The situation of her Majesty's ships* Resolute
& Intrepid *as they appeared in the Arctic Sea*
GF McDougall
George McDougall of HMS *Resolute* drew the sketch
for this lithograph showing two of the ships of Captain
Austin's squadron overwintering in 1850.

Two American ships, *Advance* and *Rescue*, under the command of US Navy officers Edwin de Haven and Samuel Griffin, joined the others in 1850. They attempted to leave again before the winter set in but became trapped in ice and drifted more than 1,000 miles out of Lancaster Sound and south into the Davis Strait before breaking free in June 1851.

The news of the discoveries at Beechey Island was brought home by yet another searching ship, the *Prince Albert*, under the command of Charles Forsyth, which Lady Franklin had sent out at her own expense, intending that it would explore further down Prince Regent Inlet than James Ross had found possible. To Lady Franklin's bitter disappointment, Forsyth decided to abort the expedition when the early autumn freeze prevented him from reaching a suitable base. As soon as the *Prince Albert* arrived home in 1850, Jane Franklin immediately began planning to send it out again. She engaged William Kennedy, a Hudson's Bay officer, to take charge, with Lieutenant Joseph René Bellot of the French navy as second-in-command. They left Stromness in early June 1851, again to search south of Lancaster Sound. Travelling by dog sledge, they made a journey of more than 1,000 miles, but although they must have crossed the route that Franklin's ships took, they found no traces of the missing expedition.

During the spring and summer of 1851, Captain Austin had sent sledge expeditions west to Melville Island and south to the coast of North Somerset, while Penny searched Wellington Channel. In an attempt to communicate with the Franklin expedition if it was outside their search area, Austin's squadron sent up message balloons, set casks afloat with messages inside and burnt smoke balls. The men also caught Arctic foxes and released them again wearing message collars. No further traces of *Erebus* and *Terror* were found, however, and the ships returned to England in autumn 1851 to share their disappointment with the relatives of the missing men and the British public.

On his return, William Penny asked to be sent out again, saying that he was certain that Franklin had sailed up Wellington Channel and that, although it was coming up to seven years since his expedition had set off, the region was teeming with animals, including deer, birds, seals and porpoises, all of which could be caught for food.

Without Jane Franklin's relentless lobbying, government funding for further search expeditions might have been refused. As well as the expense involved, opponents at the Admiralty pointed out the risk of the loss of other lives. Three rescue ships that had gone to the Bering Strait were still out – *Plover* since 1848 and *Investigator* and *Enterprise* since 1850 – but Jane Franklin insisted that it was the duty of a civilised country to do everything it could to assist its missing explorers, and she stirred up public opinion to support her views.

The Admiralty decided to make one final effort and prepared a squadron to depart in the spring of 1852, commanded by Captain Belcher and consisting of the same ships that had made up Austin's 1850 squadron: *Resolute* and *Assistance*, with the steamers *Intrepid* and *Pioneer*. This time Belcher took *Assistance* and *Pioneer* north up Wellington Channel while Captain Henry Kellett went west in *Resolute* accompanied by *Intrepid*. A supply ship, *North Star*, stayed at Beechey Island.

➤ **6.14 *Sledge party returning through water in the month of July***
Walter William May
Sledge parties would routinely cover more than ten miles per day and could be away from the ships for more than 100 days. This watercolour by Lieutenant Walter May of HMS *Assistance* gives an idea of the endurance that was needed to haul a sledge, even in fine weather. The men are wading through melt water deep enough to fill their boots.

In April 1853 a sledge party from HMS *Resolute* crossed Melville Sound and found HMS *Investigator* trapped in the ice in Mercy Bay on the north coast of Banks Island. After three winters, the last two in the same place, the crew were starved and sick. Their captain, McClure, had been on the point of ordering one of his lieutenants, Samuel Gurney Cresswell, to lead a large group of the men on a desperate 1,000-mile sledge journey to a Hudson's Bay Company post on the Mackenzie River where he hoped they would find people to supply them with food. Fortunately, though, rescue had arrived in the nick of time and Cresswell's orders changed completely. He was now to take the sickest men to the supply ship *North Star* at Beechey Island. Cresswell therefore became the first man to travel through a North-West Passage, although much of the journey was accomplished by sledge, not by ship. Soon after Cresswell's party reached Beechey Island, the steamer HMS *Phoenix* arrived with the transport ship *Breadalbane* to bring additional supplies to Belcher's squadron. The autumn freeze hampered the unloading operation and the ships had to move offshore, where

▲ 6.15 Sledge flag sewn by Lady Franklin, 1852
Each expedition sledge had an individually designed flag that would be carried by the officer in charge as he walked ahead and used by him to indicate the best route to take. The flag shown here was sewn by Jane Franklin for Lieutenant Pim, who led the party that found HMS *Investigator*, a search ship that had become trapped after entering the Arctic archipelago from the Bering Strait.

▲ 6.16 *Critical position of HMS* Investigator *on the North coast of Baring Island, August 20th 1851* W. Simpson (engraver), after S. Gurney Cresswell, 1854 This print from a watercolour by Samuel Gurney Cresswell shows *Investigator* being lifted out of the sea and crushed between two masses of ice in 1851. This was just one of a number of similar incidents that the ship survived. Baring Island is the name that Captain McClure gave to part of Banks Island.

▲ 6.17 *Sledge party leaving HMS* Investigator *in Mercy Bay, under command of Lieutenant Gurney Cresswell*
E. Walker (engraver), after S. Gurney Cresswell, 1854
After entering what would prove to the the North-West Passage from the west to search for Franklin in 1850, HMS *Investigator* spent three winters in the ice before help arrived. This sketch by Lieutenant Cresswell shows him about to lead a party east to safety. Cresswell became the first person to traverse a North-West Passage, though he did so by sledging across it rather than by sailing through it.

Breadalbane was crushed by ice and sank, giving the 21-man crew little time to climb out onto the floe. They all survived, however, and were picked up by HMS *Phoenix*, which then returned to England with Cresswell and the good news that *Investigator* had been found.

With their stores replenished, those remaining on board *Investigator* spent yet another winter in the Arctic, until in 1854 Captain Belcher decided that his expedition had done all it could and that the health of its members would be wrecked by staying out longer. All four of his ships, as well as *Investigator*, were ice-bound and Belcher gave the order to abandon them all, crowding everyone into the *North Star* and two other ships, HMS *Phoenix* and HMS *Talbot*, which had fortuitously arrived to check on progress, for the voyage back to England.

At the same time as searching voyages involving hundreds of men were going on at sea, John Rae carried out land-based surveys for the Hudson's Bay Company assisted by small groups of people with local knowledge. By 1853 only a small portion of the northern coast of North America, on the west of Boothia, remained uncharted. Rae explored a new river route which led him to divert his route considerably to the east, travelling via Repulse Bay. Returning to the bay after satisfying himself that King William Land was an island, he met Inuit who revealed to him the fate of the *Erebus* and *Terror* expedition. Groups of white men had been seen travelling southward and many corpses had been found. It appeared that some of the men had resorted to cannibalism, as many bodies were mutilated and body parts were found in cooking pots. Inuit showed Rae items which had belonged to the expedition and he bought some of them, particularly those marked with names or crests that could be linked to individual expedition members, including Sir John Franklin himself.

Rae arrived in London with his devastating news soon after Captain Belcher's expedition returned. It had to be accepted that the men were dead, and the idea of their heroism had been tainted by the horror of cannibalism. The Navy had ended its search for Franklin, and the Crimean War now demanded the country's full attention, so the Admiralty asked the Hudson's Bay Company to search the area where Inuit had said that the Franklin expedition had ended up. James Anderson, the chief trader for the Hudson's Bay Company in that area, together with James Stewart, another Hudson's Bay man with substantial experience of exploration, went down Back's Great Fish River in 1855. They found the wreck of one of *Terror*'s boats on an island at the river's mouth and Inuit showed them items that must have come from the Franklin expedition. Unfortunately, Anderson did not have an interpreter, so the opportunity to find out more details was lost. However, it was now clear that *Erebus* and *Terror* had been abandoned somewhere not far to the north.

⋀ **6.18 Sir John Franklin's Royal Hanoverian Guelphic Order, 2nd Class, 1836**
Sir John Franklin had been made a Knight Commander of the Royal Hanoverian Guelphic Order in 1836. He wore the badge around his neck, as can be seen in the photograph taken of him on board Erebus. In 1854 John Rae obtained it from Inuit, who said they had found it at a camp where there were bodies that showed evidence of cannibalism.

▲ 6.19 *HMS* Phoenix *and the* Breadalbane *at the moment*
when the latter was crushed and sunk
Edward Augustus Inglefield
In the summer of 1853, Captain Edward Inglefield, with the steamer
HMS *Phoenix* and the transport ship *Breadalbane*, went to Lancaster
Sound with fresh provisions and coal for the expedition searching for
Franklin. Before they had finished unloading at Cape Riley, *Breadalbane*
was crushed by moving ice. Those on board leapt off onto the floe and
were all rescued, but the ship sank within a few minutes.

▼ **7.1 The yacht *Fox***
British school, 19th century
Even when the official search for *Erebus* and *Terror* was
abandoned, Lady Franklin would not give up on her duty to
her husband. In 1857 she bought a steam yacht, the *Fox*, and
engaged Leopold McClintock as its captain. The search area
had been narrowed down, thanks to the discoveries of Rae,
Anderson and Stewart of the Hudson's Bay Company.

CHAPTER 7

McCLINTOCK DISCOVERS THE FATE OF THE FRANKLIN EXPEDITION

The Admiralty decided in January 1854 that the members of the expedition should be assumed dead, and their wages would be paid to their relatives up to 31 March. Lady Franklin refused to accept this and clung to the belief that her husband and other expedition members might still be alive. She felt that the search should not be abandoned while what had happened was still so unclear, but fewer people now supported her. The editor of *The Times* thought that any further efforts would be 'wasting time upon a search for dead men's bones'.

It was now obvious that the Navy had been searching the wrong parts of the Arctic for the missing ships, concentrating their efforts to the north and west of Lancaster Sound. Members of the Franklin expedition had been seen by Inuit much further south, on King William Island, and James Anderson's expedition had found remains of one of *Terror*'s boats at the mouth of the Fish River. To follow up on these reports, in the spring of 1857 Jane Franklin bought a schooner-rigged steam yacht in Aberdeen, the *Fox*, and had it strengthened to withstand ice pressure. She selected a very experienced Arctic officer, Leopold McClintock, to command the search. He had taken part in James Ross's 1848–49 *Investigator* and *Enterprise* expedition, as well as in the 1850–51 expedition as commander of the steam tender *Pioneer*, and in the 1852–54 expedition in command of the other steam tender, *Intrepid*. He had become the leading expert in travelling with man-hauled sledges, covering as much as 1,320 miles (2,125 kilometres) in 105 days. McClintock included in his team Carl Petersen, a Danish resident of Greenland, who had been Captain Penny's Inuit interpreter in 1850 and was an expert in training dog teams to pull sledges. Seventeen of the 25 members of the expedition had previous involvement in the search for *Erebus* and *Terror*.

Jane Franklin's instructions to McClintock were to search for survivors (however unlikely that seemed, as it was by now twelve years since *Erebus* and *Terror* had set out) and for records of the expedition. He was also to attempt to confirm that the Franklin expedition had discovered a North-West Passage before anybody else. Captain McClure had since claimed that credit for his route across the ice, and John Rae had filled in crucial gaps in the charting of navigable sea along the mainland coast.

The *Fox* expedition began badly. The ship did not succeed in crossing Baffin Bay during the summer of 1857 and spent the winter drifting in the ice. After returning to Greenland for fresh supplies, *Fox* entered Lancaster Sound in the early summer of 1858, revisited Beechey Island, then turned south down Prince Regent Inlet past Fury Beach to a point near Bellot Strait. Sledge exploration began from there.

▲ **7.2 The bell of the *Fox*, 1855**
The *Fox* had been built as a pleasure yacht, and when they heard that Leopold McClintock was planning to sail it to the Arctic, the Royal Yacht Squadron and Harwich Yacht Club granted him honorary membership.

During a sledge journey to the west coast of Boothia Peninsula early in 1859, McClintock met a group of Inuit near the North Magnetic Pole. They had items that had belonged to the missing expedition, some of which they had reworked into objects that were of use to them, such as snow knives.

In April 1859, McClintock and his second-in-command, Lieutenant William Hobson, set out towards King William Island. The two parties split up at Cape Victoria; McClintock went clockwise, while Hobson went anticlockwise.

In a snow village not far from Matty Island, McClintock came across Inuit who had items from the Franklin expedition. From them he bought silver spoons and forks engraved with the crests or initials of Franklin, Crozier, Fairholme and McDonald. With Petersen as interpreter, they told him about a wreck four days'

▼ 7.3 Travelling with a dog sledge, engraving from Captain McClintock's *The voyage of the 'Fox' in the Arctic Seas,* 1859
Dog sledges travelled quickly and were useful for reconnaissance. While exploring King William Island, Leopold McClintock and William Hobson each travelled with a dog sledge for searching the terrain and a man-hauled sledge to carry their camping equipment.

journey away that had been forced on shore when the sea froze at the end of the summer. The ship was deserted and they found only one dead body on board. They said that there were no longer any masts and there was little left on it, as other Inuit had carried off almost everything. There had been many books, but those brought ashore had all been destroyed by the weather long ago. The last of their people to have seen the wreck were a boy and a woman who had visited it during the winter of 1857–58. Petersen questioned the woman, who said that many white men had fallen down and died as they walked to the 'Great River', and that some were buried and some were not. Inuit had not seen the men walking, but had discovered their bodies months later. McClintock was unable to get a sense of how many men had been seen or how long ago these events had occurred.

McClintock then went to the south of the island. The coast was covered in snow, so the sledges had to travel across the sea ice alongside it.

7.4 An Inuit knife made with a salvaged British blade
McClintock bought the knife *(killuutuniq)* shown here, as well as several others, from Inuit near Cape Victoria on Boothia Peninsula. The blade was taken from a penknife made in Yeominster, England, and the softwood handle, twine and copper nails were also materials salvaged from the equipment of the *Erebus* and *Terror* expedition. Inuit workmanship had adapted the discarded items for new uses.

7.5 Sketch of the recent discoveries on the northern coast of America by Captain McClintock RN in search of Sir John Franklin, *c.*1859
Leopold McClintock and his companions found remains of the *Erebus* and *Terror* expedition on King William Island. This map locates the find-spots of human remains and personal possessions, a boat and two messages left in cairns. The messages gave the coordinates where the ships had been beset and abandoned, and McClintock plotted these. The inset shows the 'probable route of the Franklin expedition'.

At a place that had been scoured by the wind, McClintock saw a partly exposed skeleton, with fragments of clothing appearing through the snow. The man who had died was wearing the uniform of a steward.

McClintock and Hobson's searches overlapped at the westernmost part of the island. Here Hobson had found a large boat, 28 feet (8.5 metres) long, mounted on a sledge. An ascent of Back's Great Fish River would require boats, and the structure of this one had been modified to reduce its weight to make it easier to haul over land and up waterways. However, it was loaded with an amazing quantity of clothing and other equipment, and with 20 kilograms of chocolate. It also contained two skeletons that McClintock judged were of a slight young man and a large, middle-aged man. The larger man's body had been pulled apart by animals such as wolves, and both skulls were missing. There were two loaded shotguns standing muzzle-upwards and a few, mostly religious, books. McClintock noted that the boat was not pointing towards Back's Great Fish River but instead was facing back towards where the ships had been abandoned. He wondered whether the sledge team had been attempting to return to the ships.

▲ 7.6 A paddle found in the abandoned boat at Erebus Bay, King William Island
McClintock's search expedition found a large boat mounted on a sledge at Erebus Bay, with the remains of two officers inside. The boat had been modified to make it lighter and the oars had been cut down and made into broad paddles, showing that considerable preparation had gone into the plan for travelling up Back's Great Fish River.

▼ 7.7 Snow goggles
These snow goggles were found in the boat abandoned at Erebus Bay. Their blue-tinted lenses reduced the glare of the sunlight reflected off the snow to prevent snow-blindness, and the wire mesh reduced light leakage around the edges. Clearly based on spectacles, the goggles are unlike Inuit eye protectors, which were made of antler or wood with a narrow slit to look through.

➤ **7.8 Masonic seal**
The masonic device of a set square and compasses in this glass seal show that it belonged to a Freemason. So far this has provided no clue to the identity of the bodies found with it in the boat at Erebus Bay.

▲ **7.9 Shot flask**
This leather-covered shot flask was found along with two shotguns in the boat at Erebus Bay.

▲ **7.10 Neckerchief**
The boat was packed with spare clothing, including many neck scarves. This one is made of silk and printed with a seaweed pattern.

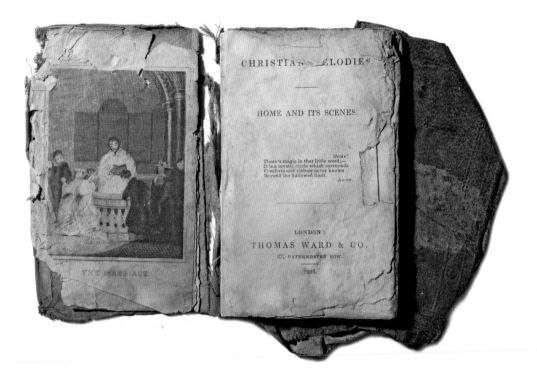

▲ **7.11** *Christian Melodies*
Thomas Ward & Co, 1836
An inscription reading 'to G.G.' on the flyleaf of this book suggests
that it belonged to Graham Gore of HMS *Erebus*. However, we
know that Gore cannot have been one of the people in the boat at
Erebus Bay, as the note left at Victory Point refers to him as 'the late
Commander Gore', indicating that he had died before the members
of the expedition abandoned the ships and began the march to Back's
Great Fish River.

McClintock named the place where the boat was found
'Erebus Bay'. Before reaching it, Hobson had found traces of
a magnetic observatory at Cape Felix at the northern tip of
King William Island, with a campsite consisting of three tents.
Hobson and McClintock deduced that the site was occupied
by about 12 officers and men from the Franklin expedition
during the summer of 1847 and that they were probably
engaged in surveying, scientific work and hunting while the
ships remained trapped in the ice. There was evidence that
the site was abandoned in a hurry, as the tents had been left
behind with blankets and bearskins inside.

▲ **7.12 Royal Marine's cap badge**
William Hobson of the *Fox* expedition
found this cap badge, known as a shako
plate, at an abandoned camp site at Cape
Felix on King William Island in May 1859.

▲ 7.13 Wire shot cartridges
Several Eley's Improved Patent Wire Cartridges for muzzle-loading shotguns were found at the Cape Felix campsite. They came ready-filled with powder, lead shot and wadding to enable shotguns to be loaded quickly. The camp appears to have been well equipped for shooting animals to provide food for the expedition.

▲ 7.14 Powder case lid
The lid of a gunpowder case collected by the McClintock search expedition at Cape Felix. It is marked with a broad arrow and the Board of Ordnance initials.

About halfway between Cape Felix and the boat site, Hobson made his most important discoveries: he found two cairns (piles of stones) built by members of the Franklin expedition, one to the north and one to the south of a bay, in which they had deposited single-page records of what had happened to them. These messages were originally deposited at the same time, on 28 May 1847, and contained the same information, in James Fitzjames' handwriting, about the ships' progress up to that time. The one in the northern cairn, at Point Victory, had a supplementary message written on it by Fitzjames, countersigned by Francis Crozier on 24 April 1848.

◄ 7.15 The message found at Victory Point
The message written in May 1847 recorded that *Erebus* and *Terror* had spent the winter of 1846–47 icebound just north of King William Island. John Franklin was commanding the expedition and all was well. Notes added in April 1848 said that Franklin had died, the ships had been abandoned and the expedition members were heading for Back's Great Fish River.

The messages read as follows:

*28th of May 1847, H.M.S.hips Erebus and Terror
wintered in the ice in Lat. 70° 05' N, Long. 98° 23' W
Having wintered in 1846–7 at Beechey Island
in Lat. 74° 43' 28" N. Long. 91° 39' 15" W after
having ascended Wellington Channel to Lat 77°,
and returned by the west side of Cornwallis Island.
Sir John Franklin commanding the expedition.
All well*

In fact it must have been the winter of 1845–46
(rather than 1846–47) that they spent at Beechey
Island as during 1846–47 they were wintering
in the ice at the coordinates given, a little way to
the north of King William Island. At the foot of
the page the following note was added, also in
Fitzjames's writing, with signatures below it:

*Party consisting of 2 officers and 6 men left the
ships on Monday 24th May 1847
G M Gore, Lieut.
Chas. F Des Voeux, Mate*

Fitzjames added further text a year later around
the edges of the Point Victory message:

*April 25 1848 — H M Ships Terror and Erebus
were deserted on the 22nd April, 5 leagues NNW of
this, having been beset since 12th September 1846.
The officers and crews, consisting of 105 souls,
under the command of Captain F.R.M. Crozier,
landed here in Lat. 69° 37' 42" N, Long. 98° 41' W.*

*This paper was found by Lt. Irving under the cairn
supposed to have been built by Sir James Ross in
1831, 4 miles to the northward, where it had been
deposited by the late Commander Gore in June
1847. Sir James Ross' pillar has not however been
found, and the paper has been transferred to this
position, which is that in which Sir J. Ross' pillar
was erected.*

*Sir John Franklin died on the 11th June 1847 and
the total loss by deaths in the expedition has been
to this date 9 officers and 15 men.*

James Fitzjames Captain HMS Erebus

Crozier also signed it:

F R M Crozier Captain & Senior Offr.

and added the following note:

and start tomorrow 26th for Backs Fish River

Dismal though this information was, it provided
comfort both for the Admiralty and for Lady
Franklin. The expedition had gone up Wellington
Channel, so searching in that area had been
justified. All was well under Franklin's command
up to the date of the message, 28 May 1847,
less than two weeks before his death and, as
the ships had not been abandoned until the
following year, he could in no way be associated
with the cannibalism that followed. It could also
be claimed that the expedition was the first to
discover a North-West Passage, as during their
futile march to Back's Fish River they reached
the coast that had been charted by Dease and
Simpson during their expedition in 1836–39. As
the Franklin memorial in central London puts it,
'they forged the last link with their lives'.

◄ **7.16 Medicine chest**
This medicine chest was found near the cairn containing the message at Victory Point, together with a dip circle, parts of a telescope, a sextant and a coffee canister. It contained 25 small bottles, canisters of pills, ointment and plaster. It is more likely to have belonged to an officer, for his own use, than to have been part of the surgeons' supplies.

In June the *Fox* sailed away from the Arctic and reached London in September 1859. McClintock's display of the items that he had brought back, at the museum of the United Service Institution in Whitehall, aroused huge interest. He described them as 'relics', a term with religious overtones, and in his best-selling voyage narrative he depicted the members of the Franklin expedition as 'martyrs to their country's fame'. The public's admiration for the heroism of the explorers had been badly damaged in 1854 by John Rae's report that they had resorted to cannibalism. The novelist Charles Dickens had quickly come to the explorers' defence by condemning John Rae for

believing what Inuit told him and declaring that it was far more probable that the survivors had been murdered by 'savages'. This racist fiction made it possible again for the British public to celebrate the heroism of the doomed members of the *Erebus* and *Terror* expedition. McClintock's account of the expedition members' resolution to brave an impossibly ambitious journey had fully restored their reputations.

Leopold McClintock received a knighthood, and nearly everyone expected that the search for Sir John Franklin's *Erebus* and *Terror* expedition was finally over.

▲ 7.17 Photograph of Leopold McClintock with items discovered at King William Island
JP Cheyne, 1859
McClintock posed for this photograph, taken at his display of objects from the Franklin expedition, holding a shotgun from the Erebus Bay boat. He asked the Admiralty to ensure that these 'relics' would be preserved and kept on public display.

▲ 7.18 Relics of the Franklin Expedition,
Illustrated London News, 15 October 1859
McClintock's discovery of the fate of the Franklin expedition was a major news story, and the *Illustrated London News* devoted a special supplement to the 'Franklin relics'. One of the images showed 'Esquimaux weapons' ranged behind products of British civilisation, as if to suggest (as Charles Dickens had claimed) that Inuit, not the British explorers, should be suspected of cannibalism.

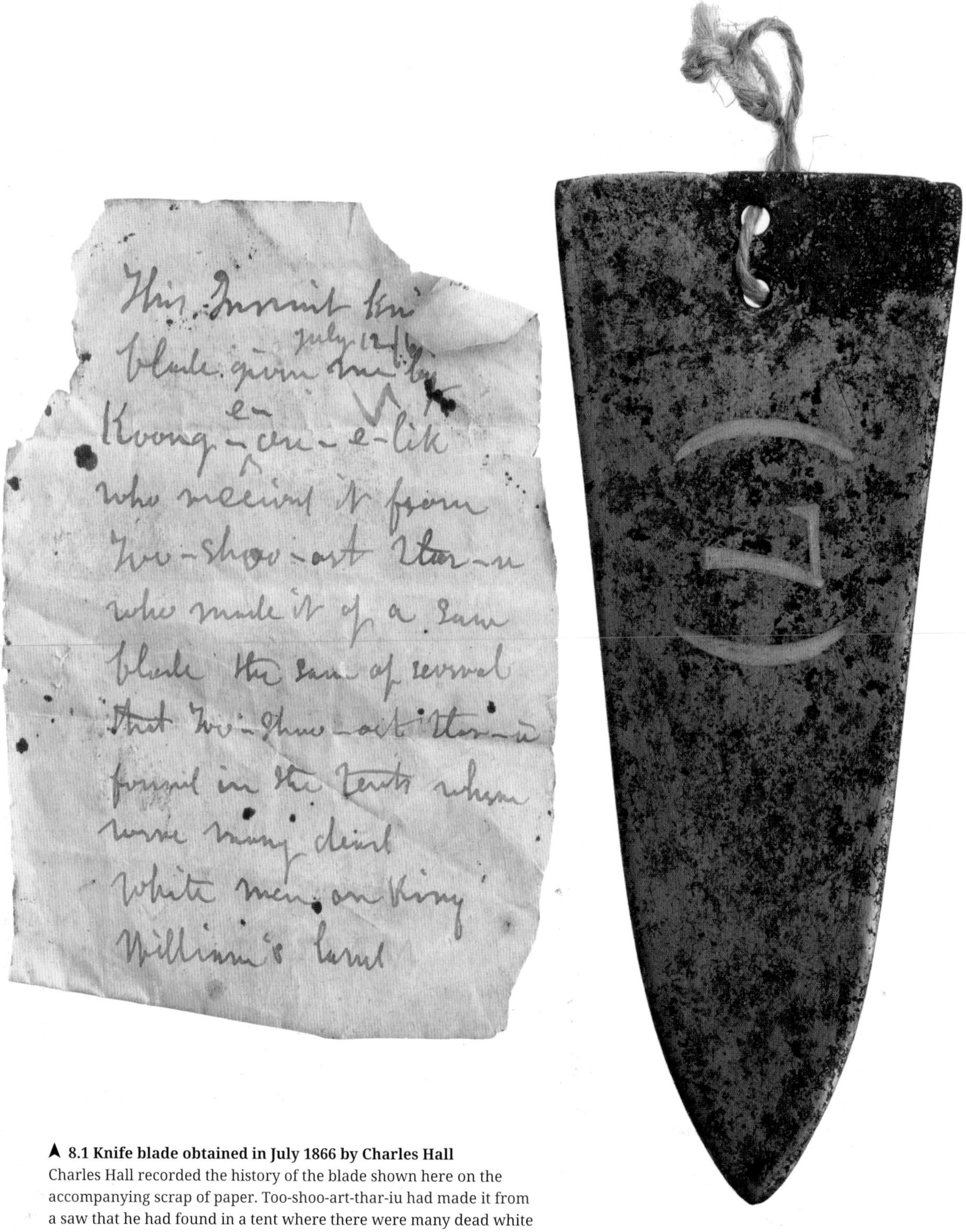

This Innuit knife
blade given me by July 12/66
Koong-e-ou-e-lik
who received it from
Too-shoo-art thar-u
who made it of a saw
blade the saw of several
that Too-shoo-art-thar-u
found in the tents where
were many dead
White men on King
William's land

▲ **8.1 Knife blade obtained in July 1866 by Charles Hall**
Charles Hall recorded the history of the blade shown here on the accompanying scrap of paper. Too-shoo-art-thar-iu had made it from a saw that he had found in a tent where there were many dead white men on King William Island. Hall also learnt that many Inuit had visited the place. In-nook-poo-zhee-jook pointed to its location on Hall's chart, at Terror Bay.

CHAPTER 8

DISASTER REVISITED

The records that Leopold McClintock brought back from the cairns on King William Island were too brief, and had been written too soon, to explain everything about the fate of the Franklin expedition. His discovery of human remains hinted at a complex tragedy. So much mystery remained that explorers have repeatedly visited the Arctic since then to try to find out more.

Charles Hall, an American, was the first of these later explorers to make the journey, in the summer that followed McClintock's return. Even though it was now 15 years since Franklin's ships had left England, Hall was convinced that some of the expedition's members would have survived by living with Inuit and adopting their way of life. He decided to live and travel with Inuit himself, talking with them through interpreters and by learning their language. He was greatly helped by Too-koo-li-too ('Hannah') and Ebierbing ('Joe'), two Inuit who had experienced nearly two years of being exhibited as curiosities in Britain and who could speak English well. His first expedition took him only as far as Frobisher Bay, nearly 1,000 miles from King William Island, but his own experience reinforced his belief that survival would have been possible.

Hall spent most of his second expedition living with Inuit at Repulse Bay, frustrated in his attempt to reach King William Island, which was still 300 miles away. Eventually, in spring 1869, he persuaded a small group to accompany him there. On the approach, they came to an Inuit encampment where a man named In-nook-poo-zhee-jook was living. He had a quantity of items from the *Erebus* and *Terror* expedition and was willing to reveal what he knew and what other Inuit had told him about the white men. Among other things, he told Hall about encounters with white men on King William Island and about some who had died on the mainland to the south. He described a tent full of dead bodies and showed where it was on a chart that Hall brought with him. He talked about two ships, one of which sank while the crew were unloading it, while another was abandoned, near Ook-joo-lik (O'Reilly Island).

In-nook-poo-zhee-jook drew a sketch map to show where this was, and the wreck of HMS *Erebus* was found in this area in 2014. He said that Inuit had gone on board this ship to see what they could find and had discovered the corpse of a very large white man (in another version there were several bodies). The ship had sunk during the following summer with its masts still showing.

➤ **8.2 Inuit map of King William Island and the surrounding area, reproduced in the narrative of Charles Hall's second expedition** In-nook-poo-zhee-jook provided Charles Hall with a great deal of information about sightings of Franklin's men and drew a sketch map to show the places he mentioned. The location marked number 1, at bottom left, is Ook-joo-lik (O'Reilly Island), where the Inuit said that one of the two ships had sunk. HMS *Erebus* was found in this area in 2014.

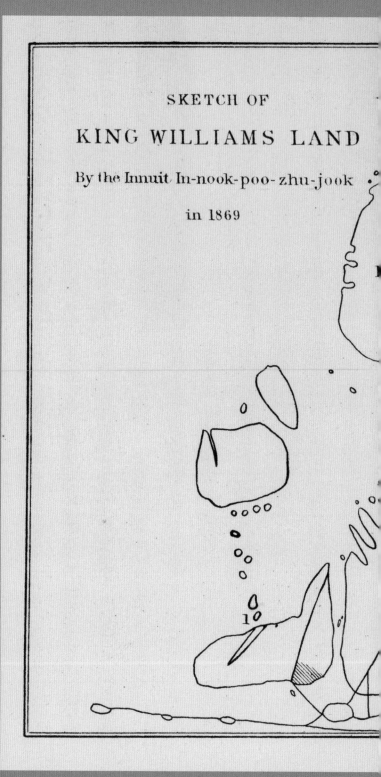

SKETCH OF

KING WILLIAMS LAND

By the Innuit In-nook-poo-zhu-jook

in 1869

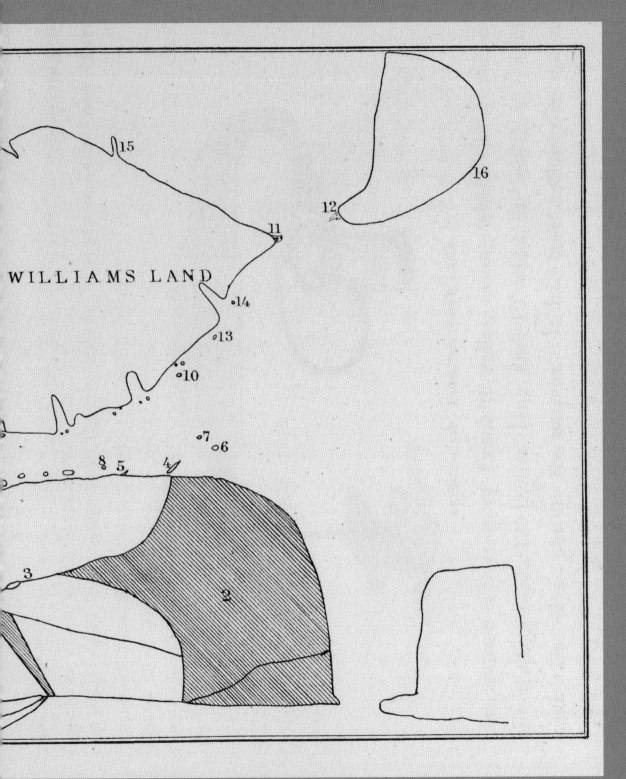

Charles Hall was desperate to find written records of the missing expedition, but was disappointed. The Inuk who gave him this matchbox told him that when it was found, it was sewn up in a cloth and contained a piece of paper. By the time Hall received it in 1869, the cloth and the tantalising paper were lost for ever.

In May, Hall set out for King William Island with In-nook-poo-zhee-jook. Deep snow covered the land, concealing the remains of Franklin's expedition. At Erebus Bay he built a cairn as a monument to 'the discoverers of the North West Passage'. He found and brought away one skeleton and calculated that, on the basis of what Inuit had told him, 79 out of the 105 expedition members who abandoned *Erebus* and *Terror* in April 1848 were reasonably accounted for. He knew that the rest were no longer living on King William Island.

A few years later, Frederick Schwatka of the United States Army heard a rumour started by a whaler that hundreds of miles east of King William Island there was a cairn containing books and other things left by the Franklin expedition. Schwatka led an expedition to investigate in 1878–80. The cairn story turned out to be a false lead; John Rae said it was one of the cairns that he had built himself. Schwatka then pressed on with dog sledges to King William

Island, on the way meeting an elderly man who had actually been on the Ook-joo-lik ship and seen the corpse, and a woman who had long ago met ten men from *Erebus* and *Terror* who were very thin and evidently suffering from scurvy.

Schwatka reached King William Island later in the summer than either McClintock or Hall had done, so the snow cover was less thick and he repeatedly came across skeletal and other remains. At Erebus Bay he buried four skeletons that were lying near what was left of the boat McClintock and Hobson had found. Progressing up the west coast, he learnt from Inuit that books or papers had been found by them, but they had been discarded as useless. At the encampment McClintock had located at Victory Point, Schwatka retrieved several items of the expedition's equipment and found a grave with John Irving's mathematics medal beside it. He disinterred the skeleton in order to send it to Irving's family in Edinburgh for burial.

◀ **8.4 Tourniquet, Crozier's camp, Point Victory**
Frostbitten hands and feet that became infected with
gangrene needed to be amputated. This surgeon's
tourniquet was used for cutting off the blood flow to limbs
so that amputations could be carried out without the patient
bleeding to death. Frederick Schwatka's expedition found
the tourniquet at the camp at Victory Point, where the
crews of *Erebus* and *Terror* had come ashore.

▼ **8.5 Sledge harness marked T11**
This harness belonged to one of HMS *Terror*'s sledges. When
it was used for man-hauling, the hand-stitched canvas strap
ran diagonally across a man's shoulder and the wooden
toggles, originally at both ends, attached it to the sledge.
It was left behind at the camp at Victory Point, perhaps
because one end was broken, and was found by Schwatka's
expedition in 1879.

➤ **8.6 Part of a boat abandoned at Erebus Bay,
King William Island**
Frederick Schwatka rediscovered the remains of the
boat that had originally been found during McClintock's
expedition. In the intervening 20 years, most of the boat and
its contents, including the two skeletons, had been scattered.
Schwatka brought away the large piece of the boat's keel
and stem shown here, as well as a sledge runner that the
boat had been resting on.

Returning to the mainland, members of Schwatka's party examined Starvation Cove near where Back's Fish River enters the sea. This was intended to be the escape route when *Erebus* and *Terror* were abandoned, but Inuit said that more than ten white men had died there.

Starvation Cove was visited more than 40 years later by the Danish explorer Knud Rasmussen, during his Fifth Thule Expedition in the 1920s, in which he became the first person to cross the North-West Passage from Hudson Bay to the Bering Strait by dog sledge. The story of Franklin's doomed expedition had certainly not been forgotten by this time, and when he came across bones of crew members, he paused in his journey to bury them respectfully.

Lachlan Burwash went to King William Island in 1925–26 to carry out geographical work for the Canadian Northwest Territories Department of the Interior. He became deeply interested in what had happened to the Franklin expedition and learnt from Inuit that a shipwreck had been found near Matty Island, off the east coast of King William Island, as well as a cache of provisions on a smaller island nearby. The Canadian government donated the items that Burwash found to the Royal Naval Museum at Greenwich in 1927,

▲ **8.7 A yard hoop found on the Adelaide Peninsula**
The Schwatka expedition found this iron fitting on the Adelaide Peninsula, west of Starvation Cove. It is marked with a broad arrow, which indicates that it came from a British naval ship. The Adelaide Peninsula is close to the find-spots of both *Erebus* and *Terror*.

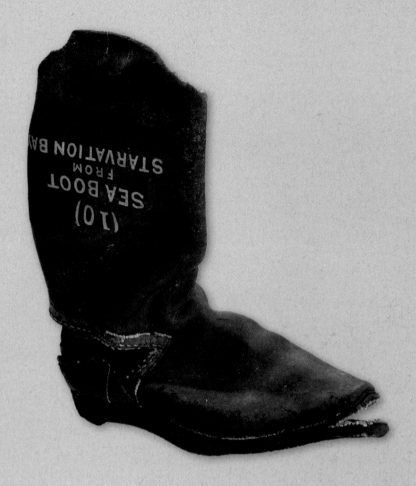

**▲ 8.8 A sea boot found
at Starvation Cove**
Members of Schwatka's expedition
heard that a boat and skeletons had
been seen near Starvation Cove, and
they found this sea boot and other
scraps of clothing. The dilapidated
boot is a poignant relic, suggesting
the worn-out condition of the men,
no longer in a fit state to walk to safety.

and Burwash prompted Rupert Gould, a researcher contracted to
the British Admiralty Hydrographic Department, to collate all the
information about the Franklin relics on a chart. Gould included
information obtained from Inuit but warned that it 'probably is not
altogether trustworthy'. The true value of Inuit testimony was not
fully appreciated until much later.

Burwash and Gould speculated that after the ships were abandoned,
HMS *Erebus* might have drifted round the south coast of King
William Island and that at least some of the wreck had come to
rest against Matty Island. On Gould's chart, HMS *Terror* is shown
as having sunk somewhere to the north of O'Reilly Island, with
some wreckage drifting west. This hypothesis stood for the best
part of a century, until the discovery of the ships underwater in
2014 and 2016.

◀ **8.9 Burying members of the Franklin expedition at Starvation Cove**
In 1924 Knud Rasmussen from Denmark travelled across the North-West Passage from Hudson Bay to the Bering Strait by dog sledge. At Starvation Cove he came across bones of members of the Franklin expedition, which he buried, and he marked the site by building a cairn. He then ceremonially flew the Union Jack and the Danish flag, attached to an oar.

BOOTHIA

PENINSULA

C.Nicholas

C.Francis

C.Adelaide

Kent P.

*'Erebus's Terror beset
in this vicinity
Sept. 12th 1846.*

Clarence

C.Victoria

C.Gloucester

Oscar
Bay

C.Sussex

*Posn. of 'Erebus's Terror'
June 1847.*

JAMES ROSS STRAIT

Is.

C.Maria dd.
Gloria

Josephine Bay

Artis.

Halkett I.

Observation Cairn
(S)

C.Felix

Cairn
(McC & S)

Cairn
(McC)

Cairns
(S)

C.Sydney

Parry Pt.

C.Sophia

C.Sabine

Tennent
I.

Blenky
Is.

*'Erebus's Terror'
abandoned here
April 22nd 1848.*

Wall B.

C.Maria Louisa

C.Porter

VICTORIA STRAIT

(Cairn)

Humboldt
Ch.

Wellington Str.

Matty
I.

C.Hardy

*Wreck (possibly 'Erebus')
repd. 1926. (B)*

Beverley Is.

Relics cached
by Eskimo (S)

Records buried (H)

Camp. Many relics (McC) Record.
Grave of Lt. J. Irving. ('Terror') Body
subsequently buried in Edinburgh.

Victory Pt.

C.Jane Franklin

Back Bay

Thompson Pt.

C.Edgeworth

Relics (B)

Melville Is.

Admiralty I.

Driftwood Pt.

Franklin Pt.

Copy of Record
(McC)

Grave & Skeleton
(S)

Grover
Bay

KING

C.Norton

Peel
Inlet

La Trobe B.

C.Porter

Balfour I.

De La

Le Vesconte Pt.

Grave & skeleton (S)

WILLIAM

Mt. Matheson

RAE
STRAIT

Colville

**Erebus
Bay**

Little Pt.

Grave & skeleton (S)

ISLAND

Luigi d'Abruzzi
Pt.

Stanley I.

Dryden

C.Crozier

Boat, 2 skeletons & relics (McC & S)
A second boat several skeletons
& relics (H)

Schwalke B.

Graham
Gore
Pena.

Skeleton
(S)

Terror
Bay

Camp. Many skeletons
2 Graves. (H & S)

Skeleton of Lt. Le Vesconte,
H.M.S. Erebus. Subsequently
buried at Greenwich. (H)

C.Rufter

Grave (H)

Gjoa
Haven

Hovgaard Is.

C.Adams

Irving I.

Washington
Bay

*Crozier and about 40 men
of the Franklin Exped.n seen
hereabout by the Eskimo in
July 1848. (H)*

Douglas
Bay

Grave (H)

Grave (H)

C.Selkirk

STIMPSON STRAIT

C.Herschel

Skeleton of Hy. Peglar, L.S.
H.M.S. "Terror"
(McC)

Booth Pt. (Relics in Eskimo possession. (H)

Todd I. Skeleton (H)

One ship,
(probably Terror) sunk
hereabout. A man's body
found on board.(S)
– 5 bodies (H)

Nordenskjöld I.

Smith Pt.

Grant Pt.

(S)

Relics
(S)

Gladman Pt.

C.Geddes

C.Seabrch.

Reid Is.

Tulloch Pt.

5 Skeletons. (H)

Richardson Pt.

Grave (H)

Maconochie
I.

Wreck hereabout (probably 'Erebus')
repd. sighted and kept secret by
Anderson's guides. (1855)

Arrowsmith
Bay

ble drift of
age from Terror

Wilmot &
Crampton B.

(H)

*Tracks of 4 men of the
Franklin Exped.n seen
here 1849–50 (H)*

Thunder
Cove

Relics (N)

Starvation Cove

Boat, & 35–40 skeletons (H & S)
Records brought here
and abandoned (S)

Skeletons (R)

Ogle Pt.

Relics (A)

Pechell Pt.

C.Britannia

O'Reilly
I.

Relics (S)

ADELAIDE

PENINSULA

Barrow
Inlet

C.Hay

Johnson Pt.

Mc Loughlin Bay

Stewart Pt.

Sherman
Inlet

Mc Crary
Isthmus

Pt. Duncan

Montreal
I.

King I.

Relics & remains of a boat (A & McC)
Relics cached
by Eskimo (A)

Elliot
Bay

C.Barclay

*A record possibly
buried at King Cache,
Montreal I.*

?

Irby & Mangles Bay

Backhouse Pt.

Gage
Pt.

Cockburn

◄ **8.10 Detail of RT Gould's 1927 chart showing the vicinity of King William Island with the various positions in which relics of the Arctic expedition under Sir John Franklin have been found**
Rupert Gould compiled information brought back by the search expeditions led by James Anderson (1855), Leopold McClintock (1859), Charles Hall (1866), Frederick Schwatka (1879), Knud Rasmussen (1924), Peter Norberg (a fur trader who found a skull and some clothing in Simpson Strait in 1926) and Lachlan Burwash (1926).

Searches for further clues about what happened to Franklin's expedition continued throughout the twentieth century and into the twenty-first, and are well described in Russell Potter's *Finding Franklin* (see Further Reading on page 171). Among these, the investigation of the burials at Beechey Island carried out by Owen Beattie and John Geiger stands out as having uncovered the most haunting evidence of the tragedy. The location of the graves of John Hartnell and William Braine of HMS *Erebus* and of John Torrington of HMS *Terror*, who had died early in 1846, had been known since 1850, and Edward Inglefield had opened Hartnell's grave two years later in the vain hope of finding documents buried with him. In the 1980s Beattie and Geiger disinterred all three men. In contrast to the fragmentary skeletal remains found at King William Island, these bodies had been so completely preserved by the ice that it looked as if they had died very recently.

Autopsies indicated that all three men had tuberculosis and died of pneumonia. They also had high levels of lead in their bodies, prompting Beattie to suggest that the solder used to seal the tins of preserved meat had poisoned Franklin's men and could have interfered with the officers' decision-making abilities. The interest and debate this sparked, with others arguing that the tins were not to blame and that disease, scurvy, starvation, frostbite and hypothermia were fatal enough on their own, showed that people still cared deeply about the fate of the *Erebus* and *Terror* expedition.

➤ **8.11 John Torrington**
The three members of the Franklin expedition who died during the first winter were buried in deep graves in frozen ground. Owen Beattie exhumed them in the 1980s to carry out autopsies and found their bodies in an amazing state of preservation. John Torrington, Leading Stoker of HMS *Terror*, died aged 20 in 1846 after suffering from tuberculosis and pneumonia.

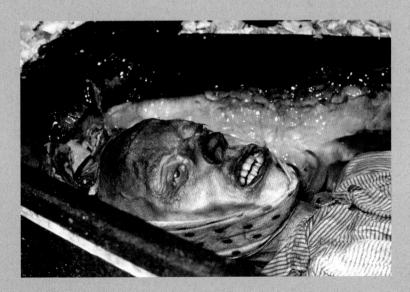

9.1 View from the bridge of CCGS *Sir Wilfrid Laurier* navigating through ice in the Victoria Strait
The Canadian Coast Guard icebreaker *Sir Wilfrid Laurier* carries out an annual Arctic patrol to maintain navigational aids. For part of that time it has served as a base for the search for Franklin's ships.

CHAPTER 9

FINDING *EREBUS* AND *TERROR*

The wrecks of *Erebus* and *Terror* were designated as a National Historic Site of Canada in 1992, despite the fact that no one at that time knew where they were. The Canadian government took the view that the ships had played such an important role in the narrative of Arctic exploration and Canadian culture that, if found, they deserved the greatest possible protection from deliberate or accidental damage.

Finding the wrecks became one of the Canadian Hydrographic Service's objectives during its work to chart the unrecorded areas of the Arctic seabed. In 2008 it surveyed a swathe of seabed 65 kilometres long, leading southwards from the main navigation channel into Victoria Strait. This confirmed that it would be safe for ships to access the area to the west of King William Island where *Erebus* and *Terror* had been in 1848. During each summer, from 2010 onwards, the hydrographers were joined in the search for the wrecks by the Canadian Coast Guard, the Canadian Ice Service and the Canadian Navy, the Government of Nunavut and Parks Canada, which is the Canadian government's archaeological agency. Non-governmental organisations, including the Royal Canadian Geographical Society and the Arctic Research Foundation, also took part.

The technology used to locate shipwrecks – side-scan sonar – requires quite a long time to cover a small area. The equipment is towed behind the survey vessel, which has to travel back and forth across the search area along closely spaced parallel lines. The operation can only take place in calm weather as the sonar 'fish' needs to stay at a constant depth, and violent snatching at the tow cable caused by steep waves could break it. The window of time during August and September when the sea is clear of ice is very brief. For these reasons, only about 150 square kilometres could be completed in one season, so the areas to be searched had to be selected very carefully.

The notes found in cairns on King William Island by McClintock's expedition gave the coordinates of *Erebus* and *Terror*'s last recorded position in Victoria Strait and it seemed probable that one of the ships had sunk near there. Inuit had reported sightings much further south, particularly in the vicinity of O'Reilly Island, and it was decided to investigate this area first. In 2010, two areas of seabed close to O'Reilly Island were searched but without success.

Meanwhile, more than 500 miles away to the north-west, Parks Canada archaeologists were also looking for HMS *Investigator*, the ship that had gone searching for the Franklin expedition in 1850,

▼ 9.2 Archaeologists leave from the icebreaker to survey King William Island

▲ 9.3 Parks Canada's underwater archaeology team: RV *Investigator* in the Alexandra Strait, the northern search area
The small research vessel used by the Parks Canada underwater archaeology team was also named *Investigator*. It was transported to the Arctic by the icebreaker *Sir Wilfrid Laurier*.

but that had become trapped in the ice and was abandoned in 1853 at Mercy Bay on the north coast of Banks Island. They succeeded in locating the ship with sonar, eight metres below the surface. Ice had carried away the masts and left the upper deck strewn with smashed timber, but the hull appeared to be complete and quite deeply buried in protective sediment, particularly on the starboard side. Video recording revealed the capstan and rigging, including rope and sail canvas, preserved in the sediment on the deck.

In the summer of 2011, a team of Parks Canada archaeologists returned to the HMS *Investigator* site to dive on the wreck and carry out further recording and assessment of its state of preservation. For nine days, teams of divers worked for 16 hours each day. They were surprised by the quantity of artefacts that they saw, including muskets, shoes and copper sheathing, and they raised a small selection made of different materials so that conservators could study the processes and rates of decay that they had undergone.

That same year, the search for *Erebus* and *Terror* continued in Victoria Strait. In 2012 and 2013 both Victoria Strait and the O'Reilly Island area were further explored, with the result that the sectors of seabed that had been thoroughly surveyed and that could therefore be eliminated from the search steadily increased.

It had been intended that the 2014 expedition would concentrate most of its efforts on Victoria Strait, close to the point where the ships had been abandoned. However, the sea ice in the strait was slow to thaw, so the vessels belonging to the Arctic Exploration Foundation and Parks Canada stayed further south, near O'Reilly Island. A Government of Nunavut archaeology team then made a breakthrough discovery of a large iron object on one of the nearby islands. It was part of the boat-lifting gear from the deck of a British naval ship, and its substantial weight suggested that the wreck it came from must be nearby. Parks Canada archaeologists began using their sonar equipment offshore and within just a few minutes were astonished to see the image of a largely intact shipwreck appear on their screen.

The ship was found to be only about 11 metres below the surface and divers were quickly sent to take a closer look. They found that the masts had been broken off, part of the stern of the ship was missing and some detached parts were scattered across the seabed.

▲ **9.4 Sonar picture of the historic shipwreck HMS *Erebus* as it rests at the bottom of the ocean**
HMS *Erebus* was discovered in September 2014.

➤ **9.5 (top) A diver views the bows of the wreck of HMS *Erebus***
The wreck of HMS *Erebus* sits upright on the seabed and is covered in kelp seaweed.

➤ **9.6 Parts of *Erebus* scattered on the seabed: diver Filippo Ronca maps a gun found near the stern of the ship**
The rigging and parts of the ship structure have been broken off the wreck by the flow of the ice and sea and lie on the seabed nearby.

▲ **9.7 Diver Filippo Ronca shines a light
on the bell of HMS *Erebus* underwater**
The bell does not bear the ship's name, but it does
show a year, 1845 – which was when Sir John Franklin's
expedition set out to find the North-West Passage.

Unlike HMS *Investigator*, this wreck was almost free of sediment but was covered in kelp. The timber was in solid condition, well preserved by the cold Arctic water, but there were holes in the deck. The divers were able to look inside the ship through these holes and could see a table leg in the captain's cabin. On the deck, which stood four or five metres above the seabed, they found two brass six-pounder guns and the ship's bell. Immediate hopes that the bell would have the ship's name on it were dashed, but it was found to bear the British government's broad-arrow mark and 1845 – the year of the Franklin expedition's preparation for departure.

The wreck was compared with the dockyard plans of the two ships, which are in the Admiralty collection at the National Maritime Museum, Greenwich. Although *Erebus* and *Terror* were very similar, they were not identical, and *Erebus* was also slightly larger than *Terror*. The team knew now that it had found Sir John Franklin's own ship, HMS *Erebus*.

Before the ice closed in at the end of the 2014 season, the Canadian Hydrographic Service succeeded in carrying out more sonar work to create a three-dimensional image of the entire wreck. Parks Canada also wanted to return to the wreck as soon as possible, so an expedition was planned for April 2015. This was months before the summer thaw would take place, however, and a hole had to be cut through the ice above the wreck so that divers could enter the water. During one of the dives, Parks Canada raised one of *Erebus*'s guns for research and conservation.

Work resumed on the wreck during the summer of 2015. The kelp was shaved off to reveal more about the structure and condition of the ship. In the final week, the archaeologists brought up a selection of artefacts from the upper deck and from an area of the lower deck that they had been able to access. These included part of the wheel, fittings from the ship, dinner plates, clothing and personal items. At the same time, the search for HMS *Terror* continued, without success.

▲ **9.8 Jonathan Moore uses the ice drill to make the second dive hole at the HMS *Erebus* dive camp**
A triangular hole was cut through the ice directly above the wreck of HMS *Erebus*.

▼ **9.9 Recovering a gun from HMS *Erebus* in April 2015: a six-pounder cannon hangs under the ice**
The ice around the hole, up to three metres thick, provided a stable platform, enabling lifting gear to be used to raise this heavy gun.

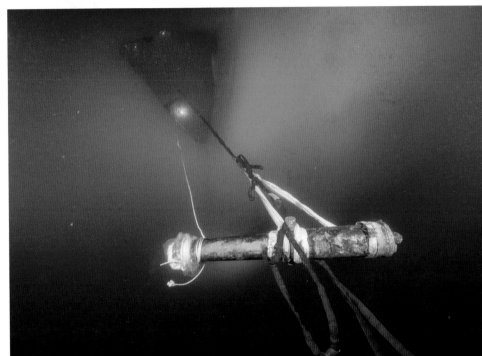

➤ **9.10 Objects left behind by the crew of HMS *Erebus*: plates resting on the main deck**
These willow-pattern china plates appear to have fallen off racks in the galley area.

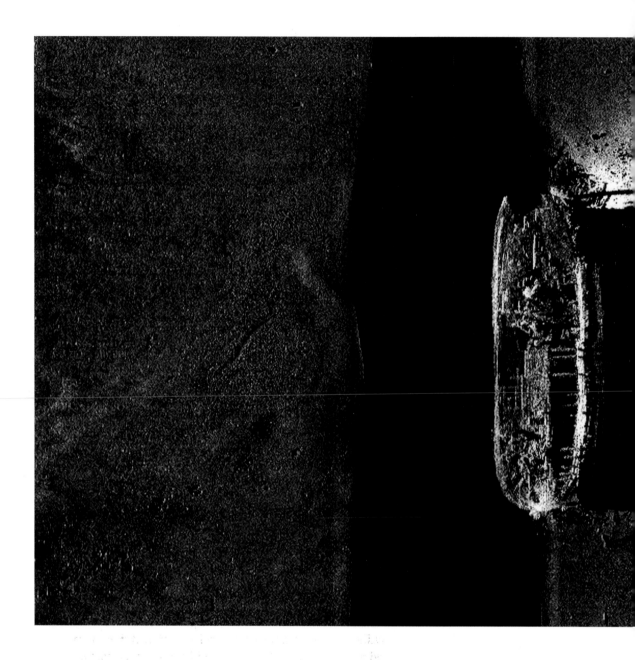

▲ 9.11 This sonar image of HMS *Terror* shows that the wreck is in excellent condition and offers hope that many unresolved questions surrounding the Franklin expedition might be answered.

The eventual discovery of HMS *Terror* in September 2016 happened far away from the planned search area. The Arctic Research Foundation's ship *Martin Bergmann* had made a detour to Terror Bay to follow up on a recollection by one of the crew. Sammy Kogvik had said that when he visited the bay many years ago during a fishing trip, he came across a thick piece of wood that looked like a mast sticking out of the ice. The *Martin Bergmann*'s sonar detected a wreck in the bay and a remote-controlled underwater vehicle was sent down to make a video.

HMS *Terror* lies on the seabed under 48 metres of water, more than four times deeper than the *Erebus* site, and it is even more intact. The bowsprit is still complete, while at the other end of the hull there are unbroken panes of glass in the windows of Captain Crozier's cabin. Both sets of davits (boat-lifting gear) were found to be in place, in contrast to those of *Erebus*, which had been torn off. The ship appears to have been anchored when it sank, and the hatches were closed. Archaeologists dived on the wreck of *Terror* three times in 2016 and assessed that it is a largely sealed environment, which could be ideal for the preservation of organic materials.

It is very apt, yet completely coincidental, that HMS *Terror* was found in Terror Bay. Leopold McClintock named the two largest bays on the west coast of King William Island after the two ships long before the wrecks were found, and he named the smaller coastal features after their officers.

Within the space of two years and two days, the long-standing mystery of where both *Erebus* and *Terror* ended up had been solved. These ships contain the last remaining clues about what happened to the expedition, and nothing in them must be disturbed until its significance can be fully understood. The greatest hope is that documents written on paper might not have disintegrated and will still be legible. This may just be possible if they were packed tightly into containers. It is unlikely, however, that any daguerreotype photographic plates will be found to have retained their images, as the surface of the copper plates will almost certainly have been destroyed by corrosion.

Having three major shipwrecks (including HMS *Investigator*) to investigate would be a challenge anywhere in the world, but in the Arctic it will be extraordinarily difficult. To help with the logistics, the Canadian government is establishing a research and conservation facility in collaboration with Inuit of the Kitikmeot Region at Gjoa Haven, a small town on the south-west coast of King William Island. Both of Sir John Franklin's ships were found through Inuit guidance and local communities are keen to remain involved in the continually developing story of the Franklin expedition.

▲ 9.12 HMS *Terror*'s helm (wheel) astern of the skylight for the captain's cabin.

▲ 9.13 Ships wrecked in the Arctic as they searched for the North-West Passage and for Sir John Franklin's expedition

Key:
1 *Fury*, 1825
2 *Victory* and *Krusenstern*, 1832
3 *Erebus*, 1848?
4 *Terror*, 1848?
5 *Breadalbane*, 1853
6 *Investigator*, 1853
7 *Assistance, Intrepid* and
   Pioneer, 1854

These three ships were not the only ones left behind by British expeditions searching for the North-West Passage or for Franklin's lost party. Edward Parry abandoned the wreck of the *Fury* on the shore of Prince Regent Inlet, and John Ross's *Victory* and *Krusenstern* were left on the coast of Boothia. Ship remains in the intertidal zone will by now have been broken up by ice and sea and probably salvaged by Inuit, but there are others in deeper water. The wreck of the transport ship *Breadalbane*, which sank near Beechey Island in 1853 after unloading stores, was discovered in 1980 following a three-year search. The ship had come to rest on the seabed at a depth of 100 metres and two of the three masts were still standing. Like *Erebus* and *Terror*, *Breadalbane* is a National Historic Site protected by the Canadian government.

Three of the four ships of Sir Edward Belcher's search expedition, which were abandoned in Melville Sound in May 1854, have also not yet been discovered. The fourth, HMS *Resolute*, famously broke clear of the ice and drifted more than a thousand miles through Lancaster Sound and Baffin Bay into Davis Strait, where it was found by an American whaler in September of the following year. The United States government paid for the ship to be refitted and then presented it to Queen Victoria as a gesture of national friendship. It is not known, however, what became of HMS *Assistance* or the steam tenders *Intrepid* and *Pioneer*. *Assistance* may, like *Resolute*, have remained watertight and drifted well away from the point of abandonment. The steamers are more likely to have sunk close to where they were left because their hulls were of a narrower form that made them more vulnerable to being 'nipped' and tipped onto their sides by the ice, which would have allowed water to pour in through deck openings. The weight of their machinery would also have reduced their buoyancy once water started to come in. As a result of climate change, the North-West Passage is now navigable in summer by small ships, and the size and number of vessels using the route looks set to increase. Unless these other historic wrecks are located soon, they may be at risk of damage due to this greater amount of traffic.

The new discoveries seem to have had the effect of telescoping time, allowing us to see the world of Arctic explorers from past centuries in close-up. Over the coming years much more will be revealed, providing new insights into Sir John Franklin's *Erebus* and *Terror* expedition and allowing a greater understanding of it.

◀ **9.14 A view across a bay towards the Franklin search ships under Captain Belcher's command**
William T Domville, RN, 1852
This calotype photograph of the search ships under Captain Belcher's command was taken by Dr William Domville, the surgeon of HMS *Resolute* in the summer of 1852. The ships were abandoned in 1854 and the present locations of three of them are unknown.

CHAPTER 10

ANSWERS AND QUESTIONS

The record that Leopold McClintock discovered in the cairn at Point Victory and brought back with him provided answers to many of the most pressing questions about what had happened to the *Erebus* and *Terror* expedition. It revealed where the ships had been and the date of their abandonment; when Sir John Franklin had died; and Captain Crozier's plan for escape via Back's Fish River. Later searchers found out – mostly by questioning Inuit – more information about where the crews had gone after landing, and they also discovered that some of the men had returned to at least one of the ships and then left it again.

The recent discovery of both ships has finally answered the question about where the vessels ended up. Search expeditions have whittled away at the mystery over the years and provided many answers about the fate of the Franklin expedition, but every new discovery throws up new questions. Some are set out here.

◄ **10.1 Sir John Franklin dying by his boat during the North-West Passage expedition of HMS *Erebus* and *Terror***
W. Thomas Smith, 1895
McClintock's expedition found the remains of Franklin's men where they fell on the march south down the west coast of King William Island. This painting is based on the description of a boat on a heavy sledge discovered at Erebus Bay. It contained two skeletons, and others were later found at the same site.

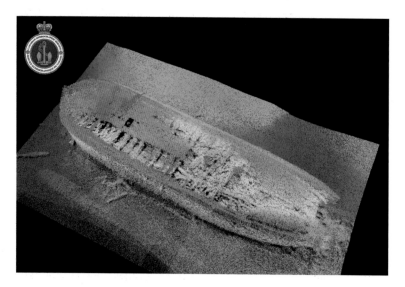

◄ **10.2 Multibeam sonar image of the wreck of HMS *Erebus***

The records found in the cairns said that the ships had gone up Wellington Channel and circumnavigated Cornwallis Island before their progress was arrested by ice near King William Island. McClintock assumed that they had arrived at that point by sailing a direct route south down Peel Channel – but was this really what happened? Franklin's orders had directed him to sail westwards beyond Cape Walker and then attempt to turn southwest. Might the ships have succeeded in forcing their way into the then-unknown McClintock Channel and have arrived at King William Island by that route? In 1982 an archaeological survey of this alternative route was carried out by Clifford Hickey, James Savelle and George Hobson. No cairns, possessions or other traces of the expedition were found, but this does not conclusively prove that *Erebus* and *Terror* did not pass that way. Whichever way they went, the ships' logs, charts and survey notebooks would have recorded it. Will any legible documents be found?

Although the ships became trapped in the ice in the autumn of 1846, they were not abandoned until April 1848. What did the expedition members do in the intervening year and a half? We know that Graham Gore and Charles des Voeux went ashore with six men in May 1847, but we do not know how long they stayed, where they went or why. Presumably they or other groups explored and mapped the island, but how much further did they travel? They were within reach by sledge or boat of the mouth of the Mackenzie River.

➤ **10.3 Direction post**
This direction post was found on Beechey Island by the William Penny Search Expedition of 1850–51, sailing in the brigs *Lady Franklin* and *Sophia*. It has a hand with a pointing finger painted on it, but what it was pointing to is now impossible to tell.

No doubt they made observations of terrestrial magnetism, but where was the North Magnetic Pole at the time? Finding this out would be an important contribution to geomagnetic science. During the 16 years since James Ross first located it on the west coast of Boothia in 1831 it could easily have moved several miles, as in 1904 Roald Amundsen found it 40 miles north-east of Ross's position. The Magnetic North Pole would have been the ideal symbolic place to bury Sir John Franklin when he died in June 1847. An Inuk named Su-pung-er told Charles Hall about an elaborate stone-built grave with a tall wooden pillar to one side of it that he had found. Could that have been Franklin's grave? The burial had, Hall was told, been disturbed by an animal and water had run through it, so there would be no ice-preserved body like the ones at Beechey Island. However, Hall was unable to find it, and neither has anyone been able to since.

Was Sir John Franklin buried wearing his Guelphic Order badge before it was taken from his body and returned home, or did his fellow officers intend to bring it back? Did they purposely give Inuit items that could be identified as the possessions of individuals in an attempt to communicate with search parties? Or is the fact that there is a large proportion of marked items among the 'Franklin relics' merely the result of the searchers' selection process?

It now seems clear that the reason for abandoning *Erebus* and *Terror* was not that the ships were about to sink, it was because provisions were running short, and if the expedition members had had to stay out for another winter they would have starved. Why did Captain Crozier decide to take the Back's Great Fish River route? Another option would have been to make their way back to Lancaster Sound, as John and James Ross's *Victory* expedition had done, in order to be in a position where rescuers could find them. But perhaps some did go back to Beechey Island, either after abandoning the ships or in the summer of 1847, as searchers in 1850 reported finding tents and a garden near a stack of 700 empty food cans, and it is hard to see how this scenario would have belonged to the earlier part of the voyage.

Crozier wrote: 'And start tomorrow for Back's Fish River'; did this mean that everybody was to attempt to make the journey? Perhaps they had to, as even a completely fit team could hardly take less than three months to travel from Point Victory to Fort Reliance, so there would be insufficient time to send back relief to King William Island before autumn. How far up the Back River did the strongest group get? Or did a catastrophic blizzard mean that nobody succeeded in leaving King William Island at the first attempt and that everyone who survived turned back? How soon did men return to the ships? Were the crews led back to *Erebus* and *Terror* by their officers or, faced with blizzard conditions on the march, did some of them disobey orders and return to the ships without them? If so, did they take over the officers' living spaces?

When did the boat found at Erebus Bay containing skeletons arrive there? It was described by McClintock as facing back towards the ships, but this assumes it arrived there soon after the ships were abandoned. Did men rejoin their own ships or did they mix up? Archaeologists may be able to answer this question from the personal possessions left behind. If they rejoined their own ships, this may suggest that *Erebus* and *Terror* were still close together, while a mixing of crews may indicate that the ships had already separated and that the men joined whichever one was accessible to them. After *Erebus* pushed on south, did *Terror*'s crew know where it had gone?

How long did the men stay in the ships? *Terror* was brought into a bay that would have been protected from the churning ice fields of winter, but when did it sink? Was *Erebus* sailed to its eventual resting place or was it carried there by natural forces? Did the men overwinter there, protected to some extent from ice movements by the surrounding islands? Or, finding their hopes to travel further south by sea thwarted, did they abandon *Erebus* for a second time later in 1848? Is it too much to hope that someone carved a farewell into the woodwork? When did *Erebus* sink?

While many of these questions may be unanswerable in the absence of written documents, there are some practical and technical questions that archaeology can be expected to clear up. Had all the coal supply been used? Had the ceiling planking been ripped away to access the coal that was rammed in behind? Where did the locomotive engines come from and had they broken down? All the other things, too, that will be found in the ships – among them, writing slates and naturalists' samples, heating systems and barrel organs – will help to build a deeper appreciation of this story of Arctic heroism and tragedy.

LEARN MORE

The National Maritime Museum collections are an immensely rich resource of objects, pictures and documents for the subject of this book. Visit the Royal Museums Greenwich Collections website at collections.rmg.co.uk. Among many other things, this museum has hundreds of 'Franklin relics' brought back from the Arctic by Leopold McClintock, Charles Hall, Frederick Schwatka and Lachlan Burwash, of which only a few are illustrated in this book. To find out about the other relics, browse by Collections – Polar Equipment and Relics – Franklin relics.

FURTHER READING

A huge number of books and articles have been written about the North-West Passage and Sir John Franklin's *Erebus* and *Terror* expedition. The following titles provide excellent starting points.

James Delgado
Across the Top of the World: The Quest for the Northwest Passage
Checkmark Books, 1999

Ann Savours
The Search for the North West Passage
St Martin's Press, 1999

Glyn Williams
Arctic Labyrinth: The Quest for the Northwest Passage
Allen Lane, 2009

Andrew Lambert
Franklin: Tragic Hero of Polar Navigation
Faber and Faber 2009

RJ Cyriax
Sir John Franklin's Last Arctic Expedition
Methuen & Co, 1939

David C Woodman
Unravelling the Franklin Mystery: Inuit Testimony
McGill-Queen's University Press, 1992

Russell A Potter
Finding Franklin, The Untold Story of a 165-Year Search
McGill-Queen's University Press, 2016

John Geiger and Alanna Mitchell
Franklin's Lost Ship: The Historic Discovery of HMS Erebus
Harper Collins, 2015

The Caird Library at the National Maritime Museum holds copies of a large proportion of the publications listed in the bibliographies of these books and is open to the public. View www.rmg.co.uk/national-maritime-museum/cairdlibrary.

PICTURE CREDITS

INDEX